Selecting and Appraising Archives and Manuscripts

by F. Gerald Ham

The Society of American Archivists
Chicago
1993

∞ *Selecting and Appraising Archives and Manuscripts* is printed on alkaline, acid-free printing paper manufactured with no groundwood pulp. As such, it substantially meets the requirements of the American National Standards Institute—Permanence of Paper for Printed Library Materials, ANSI 239.48-1984. Typesetting and printing of this publication are done by Port City Press of Baltimore, Maryland. Manufactured in the United States.

ISBN 0-931828-84-8

Table of Contents

Preface

The seven new titles in SAA's Archival Fundamentals Series have been conceived and written to be a foundation for modern archival theory and practice. Like the previous Basic Manual Series that for more than a dozen years excelled in articulating and advancing archival knowledge and skills, they too are intended for a *general* audience within the archival profession and to have widespread application. They will strengthen and augment the knowledge and skills of archivists, general practitioners and specialists alike, who are performing a wide range of archival duties in all types of archival and manuscript repositories.

This series is designed to encompass the basic archival functions enumerated by SAA's Guidelines for Graduate Archival Education. The volumes discuss the theoretical principles that underlie archival practice, the functions and activities that are common within the archival profession, and the techniques that represent the best of current practice. They give practical advice, enabling today's practitioners to prepare for the challenges of rapid change within the archival profession.

Together with more specialized manuals also available from SAA, the Archival Fundamentals Series should form the core of any archivist's working library. The series has particular value for newcomers to the profession, including students, who wish to have a broad overview of archival work and an in-depth treatment of its major components. The volumes in the series will also serve as invaluable guides and reference works for more experienced archivists, especially in working with new staff members, volunteers, and others. It is our hope that the Archival Fundamentals Series will be a benchmark in the archival literature for many years to come.

Preparing this series and volume has been a collaborative effort. SAA readers, reviewers, staff members, and Editorial Board members have assisted greatly. We would particularly like to thank Donn Neal, Tim Ericson, and Anne Diffendal, executive directors; Susan Grigg, Chair of the Editorial Board, whose good counsel and support never failed; Roger Fromm, Photographic Editor; and Teresa Brinati, Managing Editor, who brought the volumes from text to publication.

In addition, the Society expresses its deep appreciation to the National Historical Publications and Records Commission, which funded the preparation and initial printing of the series.

Mary Jo Pugh
Archival Fundamentals Series Editor

Frank Boles
Volume Editor

Acknowledgments

Many archivists have helped in the preparation of this manual. Some responded to my request for illustrative materials and examples of forms and other documents used in the archival selection process, sent me papers they had presented on appraisal, called my attention to relevant publications, and in other ways provided needed assistance for which I am grateful.

Critics are an author's best friend and I was blessed with superb ones. My first editor, Mary Jo Pugh, meticulously identified the manuscript's area of underdevelopment. Margaret Hedstrom carefully critiqued the entire manuscript and kindly instructed her old mentor. Many of her thoughtful suggestions are now in the text as are the insightful comments of Philip P. Mason, an old pro at the collecting business, who reviewed several chapters. Timothy Ericson and Helen W. Samuels helped demystify my sections on collecting policy, institutional functional analysis, and documentation strategies.

I also owe a debt to former colleagues at the State Historical Society of Wisconsin. Michael E. Stevens, in addition to reading sections of the manuscript, was continually badgered for information, illustrative examples, and copies of documents. George Talbot made me argue my way through the chapter on documentation concepts with him and was indispensable in preparing the section on the appraisal of sound and visual records. Richard L. Pifer painstakingly developed much of the illustrative material for the chapter on field collecting.

My heaviest debt is to my editor, Frank Boles for his stern editorial hand and rigorous intellect in making me explain what was vague or ill-defined, resolve what was confusing or conflicting, and reduce, if not eliminate, my sermons. At one point in the manuscript, he admonished: "The purpose of a basic manual is to tell people how to do it, not exhort people to conduct new research. We aren't out on the archival edge exploring, we're back in the center of the galaxy explaining basic concepts." I have tried to heed his advice while he exorcised my most telling observations.

I am also deeply indebted to Susan Grigg, my former student and former chair of the SAA Editorial Board, who, with the eye of a hawk, pounced on my ambiguities and inconsistencies and improved my usage of the language. The SAA Office staff provided important support, particularly Managing Editor Teresa Brinati, who shepherded the manuscript through to publication, and Photographic Editor Roger Fromm, who selected many of the manual's pictorial illustrations on the shortest of notice.

My debts to my wife Elsie in preparing this manual are innumerable. Most of all, as a former editor and eternal grammarian, she tried to make sure I presented myself to the profession as one who is syntactically correct.

F. Gerald Ham

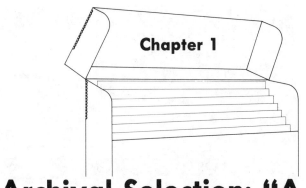

Chapter 1

Archival Selection: "A Most Demanding Task"

In the 1986 Society of American Archivists' report, *Planning for the Archival Profession*, archivists declared that their first responsibility was the "selection of records of enduring value." All other activities hinge on the "ability to select wisely." Archivists everywhere agree selection is their most "intellectually demanding task." It is not a responsibility they take lightly for they know the quality and character of the historical record of the future depends upon the soundness of their judgment and the keenness of their perceptions about what should constitute that record. Archivists believe informed and wise selection will provide future generations with a useful record of past human activity. Conversely, biased and limited views of the workings of society can lead to narrow and uninformed decisions that distort the record of the past. What makes archival selection so critical is its finality. Because archival materials are usually unique, the archivist's decision about what to save and what to destroy, or to ignore and thereby assign to eventual loss, is irrevocable. The book the librarian decides not to buy will not be lost to society but the records the archivist does not retain are gone forever. Archival selection is an act of writing history.

Why We Preserve Records

Archives are a hallmark of a civilized society. They document human experience and serve as civilization's collective memory. Preserved records transmit our cultural heritage from generation to generation. Archives are essential to scholarly inquiry into the past by historians, sociologists, demog-

Monographs based on research in archival sources are one result of the selection process. (*Amistad Research Center, Tulane University*)

raphers, geographers and others. "No other type of materials tells us as much about the past as the documents in which the actors of an earlier era recorded their doings, their thoughts, their actions, and their reactions."[1] Society relies on scholars who use these records to make the past relevant to the present.

The uses to which archives can be put, however, go beyond scholarly inquiry. Archival records have broad administrative, legal, and social uses. Archives have importance for the individual, for the community, for corporate organizations, and for society as a whole. Archives even have importance for

---

[1] Philip C. Brooks, *Research in Archives: The Use of Unpublished Primary Sources* (Chicago: University of Chicago Press, 1969), 1.

people who never use them. Records protect rights, privileges, and property of individuals by establishing citizenship, ownership of property, eligibility for benefits, and participation in public life. Records enable individuals to trace their family history and to gain the satisfaction that comes from pursuing and understanding their own personal heritage.

Historical records have much the same importance for the community as they do for the individual. They provide a sense of time and place and educate the citizenry about the role of the local community in a larger state and national context. For corporate institutions such as government, business, and education, records provide the context needed to inform and support policy formulation and decision making. Records provide perspective on program development and continuity in implementation. Records also support internal research and program evaluation. They provide important legal protection and establish fiscal and administrative responsibility.[2]

What Is Archival Selection?

Archival selection is a process by which archivists identify, appraise, and accession records of enduring value that fulfill their institution's legal mandate or other acquisition goals. The process should be:

• controlled by the archival repository's legal mandate or acquisition/collecting policy, which defines the information—in terms of functions, activities, or subjects—the institution is directed or elects to acquire;

• implemented by a strategy or plan that enables archivists to identify appropriate sources that document those functions, activities, or subjects; and

• completed by an analytical appraisal of the records and subsequent accessioning by the repository of those with sufficient long-term value to merit preservation.[3]

This selection process should govern the acquisition program at every type of archival agency from the

[2] For a fuller discussion on the uses of archives, see James M. O'Toole, *Understanding Archives and Manuscripts* (Chicago: Society of American Archivists, 1990), 23–25, and New York State Historical Records Advisory Board, *Toward a Usable Past: Historical Records in the Empire State* (Albany: New York State Historical Records Advisory Board, 1984), 19–23.

[3] The author is indebted to Frank Boles in association with Julia Marks Young, *Archival Appraisal* (New York: Neal-Schuman Publishers, Inc., 1991) for many of the ideas expressed in this manual about the selection process.

These records from a university president's office portray the age of archival abundance. The lone document case contains the surviving records of the first 60 years, while the records on the right are the archival remains of the next 30 years. (*David Scott, Husky Photos, Courtesy of the Bloomsburg University Archives*)

National Archives of the United States to the Whidbey Island Historical Society.

Though the terminology used in this manual is familiar to most archivists, there are three key words used throughout the manual that should nevertheless be defined:

• **Acquisition.** The process of acquiring records from any source by transfer, donation, or purchase, or the body of records so acquired.

• **Accession.** The physical and legal transfer of documentary material to a repository, or the material transferred to the depository in a single accessioning action.

• **Appraisal.** The process of evaluating actual or potential acquisitions to determine if they have sufficient long-term research value to warrant the expense of preservation by an archival repository. (Archival appraisal is distinct from an appraisal to establish the monetary value of documents.)

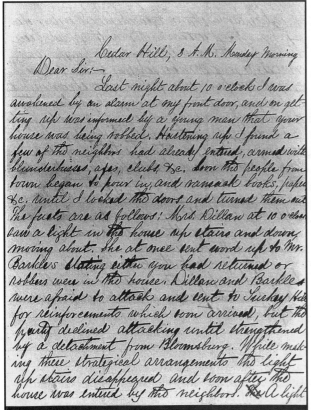

Typical archival record of the late 19th century, a handwritten letter. (*David Scott, Husky photos, Courtesy of Bloomsburg University Archives*)

Historian listens to a sound recording, commonplace among archival records today. (*Greg Booker, Courtesy of Phillips Petroleum Company*)

Why Do Archivists Need to Select?

For much of our national history, the identification of archival sources was simple. As one archivist observed, the "production of records was so meager and the number of surviving documents so scanty" that archivists "rejoiced in everything that was saved. Each and every scrap of paper lit up one more dark recess of the past."[4] This was an era of documentary scarcity, when archivists were considered keepers, not selectors. Archival administration was a custodial enterprise, and decisions about what to keep were made by individuals such as government officials, historians, private collectors, and antiquarians. Archival custodians gratefully accepted, often without examination, donations of papers and records brought to their doorsteps.

Today, archivists work in a world of documentary abundance in which modern technology in the service of burgeoning bureaucratic organizations has produced an unprecedented mass of records.

This new world has changed the archivist's role. The age of abundance has made custodianship too costly for two reasons. The first is bulk. From the Declaration of Independence's proclamation in 1776 until 1912, the federal government created four million feet of records. In 1991, it created that amount every four months. With the scant resources available for records preservation, archivists can only afford to accession a miniscule fraction of the documents generated by modern society. The second reason is intellectual control and access. Even if archivists could contend with physical bulk, they are left with the larger problem of information overload—not only how to get and assimilate information "but to determine what information is."[5]

Unable to save everything, archivists' only recourse is to abandon their passive, custodial role. Despite the protests of some archivists, the archival community must take responsibility for fashioning from this new world of recorded information a manageable historical record for the future.

Unfortunately, many archival attitudes and practices that were fashioned in the age of scarcity have been carried over to a new age of documentary surfeit. The head of a major repository urges his donors to "save every scrap of paper," contending

---

[4] David B. Gracy II, "Peanut Butter and Spilt Milk: A New Look at Collecting," *Georgia Archive* 3 (Winter 1975), 20–21.

[5] Peter Drucker, "Managing the Information Explosion," *Wall Street Journal,* 10 April 1980; also see David Bearman, "Archival Methods," *Archives and Museum Informatics Technical Report* 3 (Spring 1989), 6–8.

that each piece is "like an irreplaceable painting."[6] Many historical records are still accessioned as a result of periodic record "housecleanings" or emergency salvage operations. This kind of acquisition process is not only inefficient, it results in archivists' having to settle for the "scraps" of history. The custodial tradition, with its legacy of indiscriminate acquisition, has filled many archival stacks with what has been most easy to acquire or with what others have wanted archivists to save, often resulting in a documentary record that is a distorted mirror of our national past.

A New World of Records

The archival record was once composed of simple handwritten paper documents such as letters, personal diaries, court dockets, business ledgers and journals, and maps and drawings. In the past century, this record has expanded to include many new recording media which have expanded the breadth and depth of information once provided by traditional paper documents. Photographs, motion picture films, and videotapes capture the detail and quality of everyday life in a way few diarists or artists could. Sound recordings amplify and partially replace written minutes and transcripts. Through the use of computer and electronic formats, vast quantities of information, especially social and economic data, can be collected, compacted, manipulated, and accessed. In sum, technology has made it possible to compile a record of incomparable variety and relative completeness.

The technology that has created these opportunities, however, also has added to problems of selection by introducing acute preservation problems. The modern media upon which information is recorded are short-lived. Poor quality papers decompose. Color photographs fade. Electronic impulses become illegible due to deterioration of the medium or irretrievable because the system that created and supported the record has become obsolete. Indeed, for many of these records the cost of frequent information transfers to cope with rapid obsolescence is so high that the archivist cannot afford to retain the information.

Another characteristic of modern documentation is duplication of records and redundancy of information. Duplication is inherent in a bureaucracy. Most offices retain records they receive, copies of

Prolixity and redundancy are characteristics of the modern record. Above is a collection of nightly news film clips from local Madison, Wisconsin, television stations. (*Robert Granflaten, Courtesy of State Historical Society of Wisconsin*)

material they send, and files of internal communications or memoranda. Additional copies of such documents are often kept as information or reading files. Similarly, the files of state and local affiliates of national organizations are heavily larded with duplicate material—minutes, financial statements, newsletters, and promotional material—regularly sent out by a national organization's headquarters. Technology, in particular, the photocopy machine and computer-assisted desktop publishing, aids and abets multiplication of records.

The redundancy of recorded information is also a product of a competitive enterprise system. Take as an example the nightly television newscasts seen in most American cities, all documenting similar events whether at the local or national level. Even when the broadcast record of the network or local affiliate is unique, the activity or event that creates it is often documented many times over.

In some cases, social changes in communication, abetted by technology, have changed and degraded the character and quality of information. For example, the records of most contemporary political figures lack the intimate recorded communication and reflection—the letter, the diary, and other unaided writings on concerns of the day—that make nineteenth-century politicians' papers a rich source for research. Oral communications via modern telecommunications have superseded intimate written records. What were once the intimate papers of a congressman have been transformed into the vast and impersonal records of a congressional office bureaucracy. Once prized archival collections, congres-

---

[6] Quoted in Mel Yoken, "Collecting the Twentieth Century: Curator Howard Gotlieb," *Wilson Library Bulletin* 60 (April 1986), 24.

Information stored in electronic records will comprise an increasing segment of the archival record of the future. (*Courtesy of New York State Archives and Records Administration*)

The Province of Saskatchewan Archives in Regina is one example of an institutional repository. (*Saskatchewan Archives Board*)

sional office records are a dramatic case where the information revolution has given us more of less.

A New World of Archival Repositories

One response to this new world of information has been an increase in the number of archival repositories—more people in more places saving more records. In this manual, archival repositories are divided into two major functional categories: institutional repositories and collecting repositories.

Institutional repositories are those archival agencies that accession records directly from the corporate parent that creates the records and usually supports the archival program. These repositories are aptly known as "in-house archives." Accessions should ideally come to these archives on a regular basis through a systems approach known as records retention and disposition scheduling. The Consumers Union Archives, the Washington State Archives, and the University of Wisconsin-Madison Archives are examples of institutional repositories.

In contrast, *collecting repositories* build their holdings through acquisition of the papers or records of an individual or a corporate body from donors (who may be the creator or current custodian of the records) not legally or administratively affiliated with the repository. Many of the records come to the archives as a result of a field solicitation program. These archival agencies are commonly referred to by the inaccurate and increasingly archaic term

"manuscript repositories," or as "non-institutional archives," a term as inelegant as it is nondescript.

Most collecting repositories are a component of a larger cultural or educational entity such as a historical society, a university library's special collections branch, the local history department of a public library, or a unit of a research library. In the Boston area, the Twentieth Century Archives at Boston University, the Massachusetts Historical Society, and The Arthur and Elizabeth Schlesinger Archives on the History of Women in America at Radcliffe College are examples of collecting repositories.

Many repositories fulfill both functions, serving as collecting agencies as well as institutional archives for their parent organization. The Public Archives of Canada has a mandate not only to accession the records of the federal government but also to collect externally records and papers that document the nation's history. Many university-based repositories—the University of Michigan's Bentley Historical Library and the Mountaineer State's West Virginia Collection are two—combine statewide collecting programs with accessioning the parent institution's own archival records.

Archivists once believed that there were radical methodological differences between institutional and collecting repositories largely because of the way they selected their holdings: that one appraises and accessions while the other solicits and acquires. Most archivists now realize that the differences are not fundamental but rather those of emphasis. In this manual the two types of acquisition programs are treated in concept and in method as part of a seamless whole—the archival selection process.

Staff of The Arthur and Elizabeth Schlesinger Library on the History of Women in America, a collecting repository, examine a new accession, the papers of suffragist Alice Paul, author of the first Equal Rights Amendment (1923). (*Courtesy of Martha Stewart*)

Purpose of the Manual

The changes brought about by the age of documentary abundance have permanently altered the character of archival work, forcing archivists to become active participants in the archival selection process. As archivists are forced to select less and less from more and more, their role in determining the composition of the record of the past will become greater and greater. The purpose of this manual is to help archivists choose more wisely as they assume the responsibility for selecting the records documenting our times. Although this task is demanding, it is also rewarding and exciting.

The premise of this manual is that archival selection is an integrated process of defining and implementing archival acquisition goals. The foundation of archival selection is the repository's acqui-

sition or collecting policy, which sets forth documentary objectives. The manual spells out in detail the benefits of such a policy and the elements that should go into drafting the document that will discipline the entire selection process. The two logistical approaches by which potential archival holdings are identified—records retention and disposition scheduling or field solicitation and donor contact—are treated as parallel systems, both based on the concept of tracking records as they move through their life cycle from creation to disposition. Once potential accessions that meet acquisition policy requirements have been identified, the archivist must subject them to a rigorous evaluation to determine the importance of their recorded information and the cost of their preservation and retention. The manual gives extended attention to the criteria on which this evaluation process—archival appraisal—is based and the procedures for carrying out the appraisal and subsequent transfer of those records that "make the grade" to the legal and physical custody of the archives. Modern archival acquisition programs must also make provision for a continuing process of reappraisal and deaccessioning to make sure that only records of enduring historical value continue to be preserved. The manual offers some guidelines for this often perilous undertaking. Finally, the manual explores some of the more important recent attempts by archivists to develop both broader contexts and improved tools for the "demanding task" of archival selection.

Selected Readings

Richard C. Berner, *Archival Theory and Practice in the United States: A Historical Analysis* (Seattle: University of Washington Press, 1983), 1–72.

F. Gerald Ham, "The Archival Edge," *American Archivist* 38 (January 1975), 5–13.

New York State Historical Records Advisory Board, *Toward a Usable Past: Historical Records in the Empire State* (Albany, 1984), Chapter IV.

James M. O'Toole, *Understanding Archives and Manuscripts* (Chicago: Society of American Archivists, 1990).

Ernst Posner, *American State Archives* (Chicago: University of Chicago Press, 1964), 7–36.

Julia Marks Young, "Annotated Bibliography on Appraisal," *American Archivist* 48 (Spring 1985), 190–216.

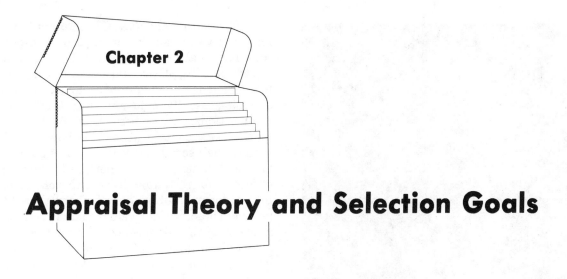

Chapter 2

Appraisal Theory and Selection Goals

Only in the past fifty years have archivists in the United States systematically put forth solutions for the problems of archival selection. Appraisal principles and standards developed from the attempt of the National Archives staff to deal with the mass of records that had accumulated in government offices by the end of the New Deal. The basic concept that underlies appraisal practice is record value. The concept hypothesizes that certain values inhere in records, that these values are primarily defined by use, and that the archivist should be able to identify and measure these values. The theory of record values is the basis of *The Appraisal of Modern Public Records,* written in 1956 by Theodore R. Schellenberg, then Director of Archival Management at the National Archives. Amplifying and refining the earlier ideas of his National Archives colleagues, particularly Philip C. Brooks and G. Philip Bauer, Schellenberg developed a systematic statement of appraisal principles, criteria, and guidelines that continues to dominate appraisal thought and practice.[1] Though conceived from the experience of the National Archives, this seminal work was applied to archival appraisal programs everywhere. Its widespread adoption and continuing use have made it the American archivist's appraisal catechism and its author the father of appraisal theory in the United States.

---

[1] T. R. Schellenberg, *The Appraisal of Modern Public Records,* Bulletin of the National Archives No. 8. (Washington, D.C.: National Archives, 1956), 1–46. This is an expanded version of the chapter on appraisal in his *Modern Archives: Principles and Techniques,* (Chicago: University of Chicago Press) published the same year.

In his appraisal taxonomy, Schellenberg defined two broad categories of record values. One was primary values, which he defined as the importance and use the records have for those who created them. The other he called secondary values, those residual uses that others, such as a historian or genealogist, may make of the record.

Primary Values. The criteria for establishing primary values are the three basic uses for which records are created:

- to support the ongoing, day-to-day administrative affairs of the creator (**administrative value**);
- to document legal obligations and protect legal rights (**legal value**);
- to establish fiscal responsibility and accountability (**fiscal value**).

Primary values are ephemeral. Though a few records may have long-term or even permanent primary value, most of these values expire when the activity or action that resulted in the record's creation is completed. For example, when a political campaign has run its course, when there is a satisfactory settlement of a will in probate court, or when the seven years of risk of an IRS audit have passed, the primary value of the records ends. For the archivist, primary values usually are of secondary importance.

Secondary Values. These are values that some records have because of the uses, often unforeseen, to which they can be put by individuals other than those for whom the records were originally cre-

T. R. Schellenberg, the father of appraisal theory in the United States. (*Archives of the Society of American Archivists, University of Wisconsin-Madison*)

ated. For instance, the primary value of probate court records is to govern the distribution of a deceased person's property, but these records are also invaluable to historians studying family wealth or tastes and genealogists nourishing a family tree. The secondary values of a record are long lasting and are the main concern of the archival appraiser.

In his appraisal canon, Schellenberg subdivided secondary values into two parts: evidential and informational values.

Evidential values. This term characterizes the information in the record in a historical, not a legal, sense. It is the value of the information as evidence of the "organization, functions, policies, decisions, procedures, operations and other activities" of the person or corporate body that produced the record.[2] To illustrate: Some state archivists will accession the director's files from a state corrections agency for the evidence they contain about the operation of the state's penal system. Evidential value, simply put, is the importance of the documentation for institutional accountability and history.

Informational values. On the other hand, informational values are wider in scope and pertain to information about the objects of bureaucratic activity: the persons, places, and activities with which the institution dealt. Some state archivists, for example, accession case files of juvenile female offenders from a correctional facility because of the detailed information they contain about this population group, such as their social and economic background. Informational values, in short, pertain to the usefulness of records for the larger documentation of American life, a documentation Schellenberg thought paramount. These broader values usually inhere in the majority of records selected for retention.

Evidential and informational values, as Schellenberg points out, are not mutually exclusive and often exist in the same records. A researcher studying changing penal theory and practice nationwide may find the files of a director of a state correction agency rich in informational value, while for a student examining the success of the institution's treatment and rehabilitation program the case files may provide important evidential data. The secondary value of a record—evidential or informational—is often a perception in the eye of the beholder, whether an archival appraiser or the researcher.[3]

Developed to meet the needs of archivists in the federal government, Schellenberg's appraisal standards have proved to be of general applicability and have been adopted by archivists in a variety of repository settings. Many archivists find Schellenberg's dichotomy of evidential and informational values useful as a convenient shorthand in analyzing and describing documentation. Others, however, are questioning his bifurcation of record value. This manual attempts to unite Schellenberg's theory into an integrated, mission-oriented concept of appraisal that should provide the appraiser with a more balanced framework for evaluating records.

Selection Goals and Methodologies

While archivists may share a general consensus on appraisal standards—the tools of the records selection trade—they differ widely on selection goals. Many archivists believe that they have a broad mandate to compile a "balanced and representative record" of society as a documentary patrimony for the future. Other archivists aspire to implement narrower institutional missions and acquisition mandates. The archives of a business corporation, for

---

[2] Schellenberg, *The Appraisal of Modern Public Records*, 6.

[3] Ibid., 22ff.

example, may have a much more restricted societal mission than a state historical society. This diversity of opinion regarding the archivist's professional duty has created tension between the concept of the archivist as keeper of the institutional record and the archivist as advocate, within the institutional context, for a broader cultural documentation. In this century, archivists on both sides of the Atlantic have wrestled with the question of selection goals and the archivist's role in assembling the historical record. Out of this welter have emerged five major documentation concepts or methodologies. An analysis of these concepts helps clarify, if not resolve, this tension. The **first** of these prescriptions eschews archival responsibility for selection, relying instead on the "unbiased" judgments of the record creator. The **second** focuses on corporate organizations and the importance of documenting the history and bureaucratic processes of institutions. The **third** relies on patterns of history and speculation about future use to guide selection. The **fourth** makes archivists responsible for providing an archival mirror for society—for identifying those issues, activities, and events whose documentary remains will most accurately represent a particular people, time, and place. The **fifth** approach, archival Darwinism, holds that given the massive and diverse nature of the current information base, a random or natural selection will provide a balanced and unbiased record without much sculpting on the part of the archivist. An examination of these five concepts may help archivists better understand the possibilities and limitations of the archival selection process.

The Creator as Selector; The Archivist as Keeper

For much of their history, archivists have been record keepers rather than selectors. Others—government officials, historians, or collectors—decided what should be saved. Some collectors and custodians believe the archival craft does not "encompass the evaluation of historical material." The most reasoned apologetic for this position was provided in 1922 by the English archivist, Sir Hilary Jenkinson.[4] Seeking an objective standard for selection, Jenkinson claimed that archivists, and particularly historians, bring to selection what they should be "most anxious to keep out of it"—personal bias and judgment. He wrote that the administrative body creat-

ing or in custody of the records was the only competent agent for making selection decisions. Even then, it should base decisions on "the needs of its own practical business" rather than purposely "producing historical evidences."

Jenkinson was concerned about the integrity of archives and their value as evidence. Archives are records produced, assembled, or received in the course of daily activity. They are unconscious and objective by-products of institutional activities. Their value is the impartiality inherent in their administrative character. Daily operation demands honest records. If, however, records were created as a conscious historical record, the impartiality and integrity of their evidence is open to question. Jenkinson's goal was an objective standard that would preserve this honesty and eliminate from selection "any motive based on alleged requirements of the future"—in short, a "representative body of unimpeachable archives." At the same time, he had fashioned a simple solution for dealing with an emerging archival problem of enormous proportion—record and information mass. He made the administrator "the sole agent for the. . .destruction of his own records" before they reached the archives, thus freeing the archivists from having to deal with "impossible accumulations."[5]

In a less rigorous and analytical fashion, archivists continue to rely on the judgments of others to determine what should be preserved. Many governmental and institutional archivists rely solely on bureaucratic rules, regulations, and directions as the basis for selection. While it is the easiest concept to use, archival non-intrusion can be a deleterious selection process. Unless the creator is a wise selector, the methodology can saddle archivists with what others want preserved regardless of its documentary value or cost of preservation. It can also result in saving what is most easy to accession. Far from producing Jenkinson's "representative body of unimpeachable archives," the methodology transmits a documentary heritage that is random and fragmentary—an epoch's documentary leftovers. Allowing the creator to designate what should be the archival record solves the problems of complexity, impermanence, and volume of contemporary records by ignoring them.

Documenting Institutions: The Dominance of Evidential Value

While most archivists today reject the Jenkinsonian doctrine of non-intrusion, many accept the

---

[4] Sir Hilary Jenkinson, *A Manual of Archive Administration*, revised 2nd ed. (London: Percy, Lund, Humphries & Co., 1965).

[5] Ibid., 149-51.

idea that a paramount selection goal is to document bureaucratic accountability and institutional history. Though Schellenberg's ideas were fashioned to fit the Washington bureaucracy, archivists have found them—particularly, his cogent scheme of evidential value—to be powerful selection tools applicable to all types of institutions and organizations. As a result, the concept of evidential value has come to dominate record selection in most institutional archives.

For archivists, the selection of records in terms of their evidential value has many advantages. Evidential value as a documentation concept is broadly understood. It is easy to put into operation. The method of determining evidential value is objective, the criteria are explicit, and the unit of analysis—the record group and series—is manageable. Through a functional analysis of an organization, the archivist can determine the most important aspects of executive direction and institutional activity and select a small core of documentation that reflects these aspects from a great mass of records.

Critics charge that the predominance of this concept in institutional records selection has led archivists to overvalue documentation regarding the anatomy of bureaucratic organizations while partially blinding them to a broader documentary heritage. The archivist by training and experience, so Michael Cook argues, has a proclivity to overvalue "the materials for the institutional history of an organisation" when they should be "concentrating instead on identifying and preserving records which give useful information on relevant subjects." By slavishly applying evidential criteria without an analysis of an office's or agency's larger societal role, archivists, so Leonard Rapport claims, have filled their shelves with records of which "probably 90 percent or more have...never been looked at by a human eye." To some critics, Schellenberg's insightful categories of functional documentation have been converted into a rigid formula for records selection. In practice, appraisal is reduced to implementing copycat disposition lists—canned solutions. This mechanistic approach has put institutional records selection in an intellectual straitjacket.[6] Those archivists who advocate selection in a broader context find this critique telling; those archivists whose narrower

Trends in historiography are of great importance to Meyer H. Fishbein. (*Archives of the Society of American Archivists, University of Wisconsin-Madison*)

selection of records is legitimated by their institutional acquisition mandates dismiss it as irrelevant.

Selection Guided by Patterns of History and Use

For many archivists, especially those in collecting repositories, institutional selection has a broader cultural purpose. Long before Schellenberg's codification of appraisal theory, collectors knew that records were indispensable information resources about people, places, and things. For these archivists the goal of selection was to ensure what Schellenberg later called "a more adequate social documentation." Many archivists hold that selection should be guided by the utility of records for current and future historical studies. Selection decisions, they argue, should reflect changing patterns in the study of history, something archivists often equate with future use. "Recent trends in historiography are of prime importance to us," wrote National Archives appraiser Meyer H. Fishbein in urging his colleagues to reexamine their selection policy in the light of changing and expanding research requirements.[7]

⁶ Michael Cook, *The Management of Information from Archives* (Brookfield, Vermont: Gower, 1986), 71, quoted in Boles, *Archival Appraisal,* 11; Leonard Rapport, "No Grandfather Clause: Reappraising Accession Records," *American Archivist* 44 (Spring 1981), 147.

⁷ Meyer H. Fishbein, "A Viewpoint on Appraisal of National Records," *American Archivist* 33 (April 1970), 175; Elizabeth Lockwood, " 'Imponderable Matters:' The Influence of New Trends in History on Appraisal at the National Archives," *American Archivist,* 53 (Summer 1990), 394–405, makes a similar argument that appraisal should be driven by contemporary research trends but in a more pro-active fashion.

Where the bureaucratic approach, with its emphasis on institutional documentary needs, dominates archival selection in most corporate settings, patterns of historical research and use often inform acquisition in a collecting repository. This has been the approach of those repositories falling under what Richard C. Berner has called the "historical manuscripts tradition." Further evidence of the link between historical research and archival appraisal are the archives that have been established or directed by historians and collected material in the historian's area of interest. The Social Welfare History Archives and the Immigration History Research Center at the University of Minnesota are two exemplars of this tradition.

Successful appraisal is directly related to the archivist's primary role as a representative of the research community. The appraiser should approach records "on the Fiery Chariot of his Contemplative Thought," evaluating demand as reflected by past, present, and prospective research use.

Maynard J. Brichford, *Archives & Manuscripts: Appraisal & Accessioning,* 1977.

This reliance on the pursuit of history to inform appraisal has led archivists to measure the value of records in terms of their potential for scholarly use. Knowledge of past and current historical use to project probable future utility is a popular selection framework. This selection approach rests on intuition and speculation. Schellenberg, who had very objective tests for evidential values, found the archivist "in the realm of the imponderable, for who can say definitely if a given body of records is important, and for what purpose and for whom?"[8]

Some archivists believe that the lack of objective criteria is an advantage and that inconsistency in appraisal judgments is a virtue. Diversity regarding what is saved ensures "a more adequate social documentation," spreading this responsibility both temporally and spatially. What is valueless to one generation, another may find highly important. Similarly, a myriad of repositories—some with parochial, others with national interests, with "one preserving what the other may discard"—ensures a richer and more diverse historical record.[9]

For the critics of this approach, inconsistency is no virtue. They argue that reliance on changing winds of historiography produces a record that too often reflects parochial research interests and the values current in the marketplace of historical writing. Enduring values should not be appraised on how they "satisfy the needs of present day research, but, at best, only the needs of future research." Yet reliance on past and present research to predict future use, argues Hans Booms, is presumptuous, nothing short of "historical theology" which elevates the archivist to "the role of prophet who reads evidence and interprets signs of future events from the past."[10] Though archivists and historians have accepted the premise that past research is an important predictor of record value, they have not done the analytical studies that would test this assumption's utility for future selection. Analysis, not prophecy, the critics charge, should be the essence of selection.

Archives as a Mirror for Society: The Search for a Balanced and Representative Record

Since the 1970s, many archivists have advocated a more holistic approach to selection, one not tied to institutional mandates, historiographical intuition, or speculation about future use. Their goal as stated in the 1986 report, *Planning for the Profession,* is to "compile a more balanced and representative record of society"—to select a documentary heritage that adequately and accurately mirrors the society that created the record. Archivists, these advocates believe, can achieve the goal of representativeness through interinstitutional cooperation, and more specifically through planning and implementing selection plans called **documentation strategies** that will "foster the integration and coordination of collecting programs across individual repositories."[11]

While almost unknown to archivists in North America until 1984, a parallel but more encompassing approach had been discussed by the German archivist Hans Booms more than a decade earlier. In 1971, he set forth a program to achieve a comprehensive and representative record of society, free from the taint of the archivist's or historian's biases.

[8] Schellenberg, *Appraisal of Modern Public Records,* 25.
[9] Ibid., 44.
[10] F. Gerald Ham, "The Archival Edge," *American Archivist* 38 (January 1975), 8; Hans Booms, "Society and the Formation of a Documentary Heritage: Issues in the Appraisal of Archival Sources," *Archivalische Zeitschrift* 68 (1972), 3–40 and translated from the German and reprinted in *Archivaria* 24 (Summer 1987), 69–107.
[11] *Planning for the Archival Profession: A Report of the SAA Task Force on Goals and Priorities* (Chicago: Society of American Archivists, 1986), 10. For a discussion of documentation strategies, see Chapter 11.

Professor Doctor Hans Booms holds that public opinion should legitimize archival appraisal. (*Bundesarchiv, Koblenz, Germany*)

"Only Society," he wrote, "and the public opinion it expresses can give legitimacy to archival selection." Public opinion, he argued, is a constituent part of modern society, sanctioning public actions and legitimating political authority. Why, he asked, should it not "also legitimize archival appraisal?"[12] As the foundation for "all archival selection efforts," Booms outlined a methodology for measuring the "societal significance" of past phenomena by analyzing the value that contemporaries attached to them. This analysis of events formed what he called a "kind of documentation model" or plan. Through a series of such plans, each prepared for a particular segment of "the total societal process," the archivist would have a guide to "positive value selection" as well as a methodology "for appraising the great volume of record material." Booms' model was interinstitutional and interdisciplinary requiring cooperation among archivists and archival institutions as well as their consultation with colleagues from "different areas of life such as administration, science, the me-

dia or economics" in shaping society's documentary heritage.[13]

The American advocates of representativeness have given less thought to a grand theory than Booms, but more attention to mechanisms to assist in compiling an adequate documentation of society. Nevertheless there are common elements in the two approaches. Both hold that selection should focus first on what events and phenomena should be documented rather than on what records should be retained. Both assume the need to transcend the limitations of institutionally based appraisal and to select records in a larger informational and societal context. Because analysis and selection transcend the interest of any single archival authority, they must take place in an interinstitutional framework. Documentation strategies sculpt the historical record and demand aggressive archival intervention.

To its proponents this methodology offers many advantages. First, it provides a comprehensive and rationally planned archival record. Second, documentation strategies enable the archivist to save fewer but better records, thus maximizing resources available for archival selection and preservation. Third, the proposed mechanisms facilitate archival selection of interrelated records across institutional and disciplinary boundaries.

There are several problems with this concept. It is highly theoretical and untested in the crucible of practice. Where other selection methodologies grew out of practical application, Booms' documentation plan is an idea in search of a blueprint while documentation strategies await a successful demonstration. These models and plans require a knowledge of the information universe—what their proponents call the "universe of documentation"—and interinstitutional exchange systems for sharing information on holdings and selection decisions that archivists have yet to develop and implement. The real barriers to designing a balanced and representative record, however, are not planning and testing, but the enormous investment in fiscal and human resources required to implement this selection methodology.

Archival Darwinism as a Selection Methodology

Rather than trying to engineer "representativeness," some archivists argue that a process of natural selection will do it for us. "The law of aver-

---

[12] Hans Booms, "Society and the Formation of a Documentary Heritage," 104.

[13] Ibid., 106–07.

Natural selection, according to David Bearman, will ensure an adequate archival record. (*Courtesy of David Bearman*)

ages as it pertains to the survival of records," writes David Bearman, the major proponent of archival Darwinism, "assures the retention of vast classes of materials without further attention by archives." Bearman argues that archival methods and resources for selection are "so utterly inadequate for the size of available documentation" that the archivist is unable to consciously shape the historical record in any significant fashion. Even if there were an exponential increase in these resources, archivists, according to Bearman, would be "prohibited, even collectively, from ever coming into contact with all but a tiny percentage of . . . [the annual accumulation of recorded evidence]." But archivists can still have representativeness as their goal, for "random and accidental processes outside of the domain of conscious culture preservation" dwarf the impact of their activity. This basic reliance on a fortuitous selection process does not, however, relegate the archivist to the role of a Jenkinsonian "keeper," for archivists need to factor into their selection decisions a broader universe of information such as the retention programs of other archival repositories as well as those of cultural institutions such as libraries and museums. Nevertheless, archival selection must

"first and foremost, take into account the effects that random retention will have in preserving records one hundred years from now." Only when there is reason to believe random selection will not adequately "assure the survival of an historically valid sample," Bearman concludes, should archivists attempt to design representativeness into the "informational record." How such determinations are made, Bearman does not say.[14]

Appraisal approaches based on trying to build a representative record of human culture through actively shaping the archival record fail to make a dent in the record as it will be preserved a hundred years from now.

David Bearman, *Archival Methods*, 1989.

Archival natural selection has many attractions. It recognizes the limitations of planned selection in an age of documentary abundance. It tells the archivist to be reasonable and not pretentious in selection. It recognizes that the failure of current selection approaches requires a rethinking of objectives. Rather than attempt a utopian reordering of the documentary universe, it leaves archivists free to better fill their institutional mandates.

But it also absolves the archivist from a larger role in determining the documentary record. It provides no guidelines other than "do not worry." Further, the gaps in the eighteenth- and nineteenth-century historical record suggest that archival Darwinism may be an inadequate selection methodology. To rely on this approach, archivists need to know how to predict when random selection will not provide a representative sample.

Summary

• Appraisal theory in the United States was developed at the National Archives and codified by T. R. Schellenberg. It is based on the belief that certain values are inherent in records. Records have primary values—administrative, legal, and fiscal—for their creators. Records also have secondary value primarily for historical uses. The record's secondary value is the archivist's primary concern.

• In assessing this value, archivists are concerned with the **evidential** significance of the record—the evidence it contains on the functions and activities of its creating body over time—as well as **informational** importance of the record—what it

---

[14] Bearman, "Archival Methods," 15–16.

tells us about the persons, places, and things with which the agency dealt.

• Appraisal does not take place in a vacuum but in the context of larger selection goals. Archivists differ widely on the validity of these goals. Many believe that as members of the profession they have a broad mandate to compile a balanced and representative record of society. Others believe they best serve the larger society fulfilling their local institutional mandate.

• Selection goals are not only the product of differing institutional missions and acquisition mandates—the archivist's internal environment—but also reflect a broader, ever-changing external social, cultural, and technological environment.

• Even when archivists agree on larger documentation goals, they differ on strategies. Some hold that in today's complex society archivists must deliberately plan to sculpt a representative documentary heritage while others believe random retention will achieve the same goal.

• Whether or not archivists can significantly affect the larger ecology of the information universe—and have a professional mission to do so—they are not absolved from thoughtfully tending their own repository gardens, carefully developing program selection goals and methods. Their first task is to develop a repository acquisition policy that defines the institution's role in contributing to a larger documentary heritage.

Selected Readings

David Bearman, "Archival Methods," *Archives and Museum Informatics Technical Report* 3 (Spring 1989), 6–16.

G. Philip Bauer. *The Appraisal of Current and Recent Records* (National Archives Staff Information Circular No. 13, 1946).

Frank Boles in association with Julia Marks Young, *Archival Appraisal* (New York: Neal-Schuman Publishers, Inc., 1991), Chapter 1.

Philip Coolidge Brooks, "The Selection of Records for Preservation," *American Archivist* 3 (October 1940), 221–234.

Hans Booms, "Society and the Formation of a Documentary Heritage: Issues in the Appraisal of Archival Sources," *Archivalische Zeitschrift* 68 (1972), 3–40. Translated from the German and reprinted in *Archivaria* 24 (Summer 1987), 69–107.

Meyer H. Fishbein, "A Viewpoint on Appraisal of National Records," *American Archivist* 33 (April 1970), 175–187.

Elizabeth Lockwood, " 'Imponderable Matters:' The Influence of New Trends in History on Appraisal at the National Archives," *American Archivist* 53 (Summer 1990), 394–405.

Nancy E. Peace, "Deciding What to Save: Fifty Years of Theory and Practice," in Nancy E. Peace (ed.), *Archival Choices: Managing the Historical Record in an Age of Abundance* (Lexington, Mass.: D.C. Heath, 1984), 1–18.

T. R. Schellenberg, *The Appraisal of Modern Public Records*, Bulletin of the National Archives No. 8 (Washington, D.C.: National Archives, 1956), 1–46.

Developing a Framework for Selection: The Acquisition Policy

The foundation of the selection process is the repository acquisition policy. This policy, setting forth the documentation goals and objectives of the archival program, is essential to guide repositories in selecting records, to build collections in a systematic way, and to set limits to what is accessioned. It is the "first level of appraisal," providing a framework within which an archivist makes individual appraisal decisions.[1] Its primary purpose is to define what should be documented in terms of information—whether subjects, functions, or activities—rather than records.

> The way in which a repository defines, expands upon, and implements [acquisition policy] is the foundation of the appraisal process.
>
> Frank Boles and Julia Young, "Exploring the Black Box," 1985.

Archivists must craft coherent acquisition policy statements with sufficient specificity to make them useful. In the past, general, open-ended statements, like that of one midwestern repository that purports to collect records "of persons, events, and activities [that] capture the general fabric of [this region's] ... experiences over time," have been the rule. Such statements do little more, in the words of one critic, than "grant a repository a perpetual hunting license for records."[2] A vague and overly broad acquisitions policy is of no help to the archivist in making particular selection decisions.

In the past, written acquisition policies have usually been considered the province of the collecting archives and irrelevant to the needs of an in-house repository. For the latter, the mission, organization, and operations of the parent institution, linked to evidential appraisal criteria, were assumed to provide an adequate framework for selection. Without the conceptual framework provided by an acquisition policy, however, institutional archives selection decisions are often rote or capricious.

Benefits of a Well-Designed Repository Acquisition Policy

- Repository acquisition policy provides an intellectual or conceptual framework for rational decision-making. It guides an institution in building its archival holdings and provides guidelines against which to measure appraisal decisions. It allows archivists to sharpen their collecting focus so they can collect more coherently and progressively in a selected area.
- It is the ethical foundation of the acquisition program. It allows archival institutions to state their intentions—selection goals—to others and thus can help avoid competition and conflict in collecting. It is a *sine qua non* of interinstitutional cooperation.

---

[1] Frank Boles, "Mix Two Parts Interest to One Part Information and Appraise Until Done: Understanding Contemporary Record Selection Processes," *American Archivist* 50 (Summer 1987), 362.

[2] Frank Boles and Julia Marks Young, "Exploring the Black Box: The Appraisal of University Administrative Records," *American Archivist* 48 (Spring 1985), 137.

• It enables archivists more easily to explain to records custodians and donors why their records are significant and how they complement existing holdings.

• It provides specific criteria for rejecting unsolicited collections. Thus, it is an essential buffer between the archivist and those who would force unwanted collections on the archives. It can prevent archivists from wasting time going after what they do not want and allow the archival institution to reject gracefully what it should not collect.

• It provides a strong justification for the hazardous and emotionally charged process of reappraising and deaccessioning collections that are out-of-scope or earlier accessions of little value.

• It gives continuity to the acquisition program with changes in administration and staffing.

• It enables repositories to make wiser use of limited resources by bringing collecting in line with resources available for preservation, storage, and use. It recognizes that there are "opportunity costs" associated with acquisition decisions.

Some Factors to Consider in Developing an Acquisition Policy

A useful acquisition policy is not based on generality, whimsy, or preconception but upon careful analysis, within the framework of the institutional mandate, of the goals of the acquisition program and the resources to support it. The following analysis, while essential for building and improving collecting repository programs, is also important for developing institutional archives.

Archivists must first examine the *availability of institutional resources*. Will the policy be too big for the warehouse? What staff, physical facilities, and other resources will be needed to support the acquisition, processing, preservation, and use of the records, and are such resources available or likely to be forthcoming? It is ethically irresponsible for the repository to accession what cannot be preserved under proper conditions of storage and made available for use. It is also irresponsible for a repository to become so overcommitted that it stops accepting additional installments to established collections.[3] The warehouse can, however, be expanded. Archivists need to plan not only for acquiring better records but also for the resources to take care of them. In tailoring acquisitions to resources, the archivist

needs to assess carefully future resource development.

The wise archivist will also examine the *availability of information*. Is the information the repository wants to preserve available in existing records that can be accessioned? It is foolish to attempt to acquire what is not accessible.

The *availability of related materials* is an equally important consideration. Does the repository or its parent institution have the complementary primary and secondary materials—books, pamphlets, periodicals, newspapers—necessary to support general research use of the archival holdings?

Equally essential is a knowledge of *related or parallel acquisition efforts*. The archivist should know in detail the acquisition design and holdings of other repositories with a parallel or closely related acquisition focus that can supplement, limit, or otherwise help define the policy. The need for this analysis should be self-evident to collecting institutions, but it also can benefit those in-house archives concerned with documentary redundancy and interested in coordinating their acquisition efforts and holdings with related institutions to produce a more useful and less parochial historical record.

Archivists also need to *analyze current holdings* of their own repository to assay the collection's strengths and weaknesses. A policy based on such an assessment can guide the repository in adding appropriate new material.

Tools for Formulating Acquisition Policies and Plans: Collection Analysis and Functional Analysis

Collection Analysis. A number of archivists in different institutional settings are using a new archival tool called collection analysis to gather and evaluate information on some of the above factors. Developed by librarians, the archival collection analysis process involves evaluating the topical and quantitative characteristics of repository holdings for use as a measure in developing acquisition priorities. The process has two phases: the **first,** using survey techniques, involves the enumeration of specific characteristics of a repository's holdings such as subject, geographic, or chronological coverage, and record quantity or type. The **second** is a qualitative evaluation of the findings to provide an assessment of the strengths and weaknesses of a repository's holdings. In this second phase, archivists also evaluate acquisition possibilities in specific collecting areas and analyze how well specific fields are docu-

────────────

[3] Philip P. Mason, "The Ethics of Collecting," *Georgia Archive* 5:1 (Winter 1977), 45–47.

mented either in other repositories or in non-archival information sources. This process, linking analysis to policy formulation, provides a conceptual framework in which the archivist can more systematically determine collecting focus and priorities. This process has been applied in statewide, regional, and local settings. The reader will find an example of a collection analysis summary for the field of religion in Figure 3-2.[4]

Institutional Functional Analysis. For those archivists whose responsibility is documenting the institution they work for, a tool, which its designer Helen Samuels calls *institution functional analysis,* can provide the background information they need to formulate collection policies and select records. An outgrowth of Samuels' work with documentation strategies, functional analysis is an examination at the **institutional level** of what an organization **does** rather than a structural analysis of who does it. This level of analysis "is required to understand the nature of modern institutions and the broad range of activities that it encompasses." The process involves a study of the functions of each unit in an institution and an evaluation of its importance to the institution.

The archivist then translates this information into a detailed documentation plan, using more familiar archival tools. The first step is to prepare brief administrative histories of each unit in the organization to give the archivist an understanding not only of what is to be documented but what documentation is sought. The second step is to conduct a collection analysis to determine the adequacy of current archival holdings. The archivist must also identify and evaluate information not in the archives— whether it is found in unpublished records, published materials, aural or visual records, or even artifacts—for its value as potential evidence of particular functions and activities. Archival principles, particularly provenance, will determine how those records are located. With the information gained from the above steps, the archivist can formulate a detailed documentation plan—in effect, the acquisition policy for

the institution.[5] Institutional functional analysis, according to Samuels, can make clear the full breadth of an institution's activities that need to be documented and thus enable archivists to select more intelligently from abundant records as well as to plan ways to document those functions that create few records.

Drafting the Acquisition Policy

Every institution's acquisition policy must be custom tailored. There are, however, a few basic components that should be common to all policies. These include (1) a statement of institutional mission and purpose; (2) a field-by-field delineation of collecting scope and priorities; (3) acquisition guidelines and limitations; (4) types of cooperation with other repositories and records custodians; and (5) a deaccessioning statement. The repository also needs a procedure to monitor and update the policy.[6]

1. The statement of repository mission and purpose. This is the policy's foundation and should set forth both the general scope of the acquisition program and the legal or administrative authority on which it rests. It also should clearly state the purpose of the repository. In Faye Phillips' words, this statement "must be in agreement with and flow from that of the institution of which it is a part." This statement may be a specific statutory mandate to a state archives or other public historical agency, a directive from a corporation's chief executive officer, rules and regulations adopted by a university's board of regents, or a charge contained in a private historical society's corporate charter. A repository should reexamine its existing mission statement. Is it still relevant in light of changing internal and external conditions? Is it sufficiently limited and specific? Does it need to be scaled back in line with available resources? An unrealistic mission statement renders the acquisition policy useless. The mission may support a program of broad social and economic documentation or mandate a circumscribed acquisition program primarily designed for the legal protection of the institution, but whatever the scope, the particulars of the acquisition program are founded in the mission.[7] Though many repositories still operate

---

[4] For a description of this methodology, see Judith E. Endelman, "Looking Backward to Plan for the Future: Collection Analysis for Manuscript Repositories," *American Archivist* 50 (Summer 1987), 340–55, and State Historical Society of Wisconsin, "Collection Development Policy for Wisconsin Manuscripts," (Madison, 1986), Appendix D. See Christine Weideman, "A New Map for Field Work: Impact of Collections Analysis on the Bentley Historical Library," *American Archivist* 54 (Winter 1991), 54–60, for a case study of how this process improved the repository's collecting program.

[5] For a detailed description of institutional functional analysis, see Helen W. Samuels, *Varsity Letters: Documenting Modern Colleges and Universities* (Metuchen, N.J.: Scarecrow Press, Inc., and Society of American Archivists, 1992), 1–18.

[6] The standard article on policy development and content is Faye Phillips, "Developing Collecting Policies for Manuscript Collections," *American Archivist* 47 (Winter 1984), 30–42.

[7] Boles and Young, "Exploring the Black Box," 137.

with an unwritten mission, fashioned by tradition, archival agencies need to codify a written statement of mission and purpose. (See Figure 3-1.)

2. Delineating the scope and focus of collecting: acquisition fields. Defining collecting fields and/or subfields within the larger collecting institutional mandate is the heart of the acquisition policy. These fields may be defined in several alternate ways. The most common field is defined by *subject.* The State Historical Society of Wisconsin's policy for statewide collecting is organized by sixteen subject categories such as arts, communications, organized labor, and recreation/leisure. Acquisition fields are also defined by *provenance*—who created, accumulated, and maintained the records—such as state and local government agencies, legislative bodies, or social and service organizations. Institutions may define fields by *function and activities.* For example, *Varsity Letters* lists seven major functional fields common to college and university archives including teaching, research, governance and funding, and student life. The Florida State Archives policy also defines fields by *type of records* such as photographs, moving images, and sound recordings. The acquisition fields often need to be further defined by *geographical area*—urban or rural; or by region, state or locality—and by the *time period* that will be documented for a particular activity or subject.

For each collecting field, the policy may include a brief analytical statement of the strengths and weaknesses of current holdings based on the collection analysis or functional study. This statement might also include related published research materials as well as collateral materials held by other institutions.

Within each field the policy should identify specific functions or topics—groups, events, or issues—to be documented as well as the priority and level of collecting activity necessary to strengthen the holdings in the field.

3. Acquisition guidelines: priorities and limitations. The policy should establish guidelines for setting priorities and levels of acquisition activity, stipulating conditions governing acquisition and retention, and stating what limitations or conditions the institution may impose on those collections that are within the scope of the policy.

Acquisition priorities. The archivist should establish priorities for the fields and sub-fields listed in the policy. Criteria for establishing acquisition priorities for specific fields include:

- the importance of the function or subject in relationship to the repository's mission and purpose

- the extent to which the function or subject is documented in existing repository holdings

- the extent to which the function or subject is adequately documented in non-archival sources, such as newspapers, periodicals, government publications, books, and other publications

- the holdings and acquisitions programs of other repositories in the same functional or collecting field

- the risk that the records will be lost if they are not accessioned in a timely fashion

- a demonstrated or anticipated need by researchers for additional documentation on the subject.

In general, new acquisitions should add substantive documentation, rather than simply provide more information about subjects that already are well-documented in a repository's holdings. These criteria, of course, must be evaluated in the framework of the collecting mandate. For example, for some repositories, criteria such as anticipated use by researchers or parallel information resources held elsewhere are irrelevant to their institutional mission.

Levels of acquisition activity. Using these criteria, the repository can assign to each field and subfield enumerated in the policy a level of acquisition activity. An example is the collection policy on the next page which divides the intensity of its acquisition efforts into two categories: *solicitation* and *acceptance.* The highest level, *solicitation,* involves the active identification and acquisition of records of greatest importance. Solicitation is appropriate for under-documented areas or fields in which the repository strives for a more comprehensive record. *Acceptance* is an appropriate level for fields that may need strengthening but are already represented in the repository's holdings, documented by non-archival resources, or where a representative rather than comprehensive documentation is desired. At this level, identification and acquisition are pursued as time and opportunity permits. (See Figure 3-2.)

Acquisition guidelines also need to spell out other matters such as the conditions the repository places on the acceptance of a donation; the disposition of unwanted materials the repository staff removes from an accession; classes of materials the

Figure 3-1   Mission Statement

> **Mission of the Archives.** The primary purposes of the University of Wisconsin-Madison Archives are: to preserve University records and information of permanent historical value; to provide records management services; and to serve as an educational resource encouraging administrative and scholarly research in its collections. As part of General Services, the University Archives reports to the Vice Chancellor for Academic Affairs. Its governing policies are approved by the campus Archives Committee (Faculty Policies and Procedures 6.20). Operating policies and procedures employed to carry out the mission of the Archives are based on the "Core Mission and Minimum Standards for University Archives in the University of Wisconsin System," endorsed by the Board of Regents in 1980.
>
> In carrying out its mission the University Archives:
>
> A) is an official state depository of records. In 1985 the Archives was designated as the official depository for all records of permanent value of the UW-Madison, the System Administration, the UW-Extension, and the Center System.
>
> B) develops, maintains and distributes a manual which outlines procedures for offices to meet their responsibilities for records management and preservation and to gain access to University and State records services.
>
> C) in consultation with appropriate campus offices, provides efficient and economical records management services; determines administrative, financial, legal and historical records preservation needs within the University; and serves as intermediary between University offices and the State of Wisconsin Public Records and Forms Board.
>
> D) appraises, accessions, arranges, describes and preserves records transferred to its custody while providing access to its holdings, in accordance with accepted professional archival principles.
>
> E) cooperates with state and national archival, historical and records management professional organizations on behalf of the University to keep informed on major issues of concern to the profession and participates in networking arrangements to share resources with other research institutions.
>
> *Courtesy of University of Wisconsin-Madison*

repository will not accept; and any provision for making exceptions to the policy.

Conditions of acceptance. These conditions generally involve such matters as ownership, restrictions on access, demands on repository resources, and financial arrangements and benefits provided by the donor. The policy should prohibit acceptance of records where the right of the custodian or donor to legally transfer ownership of the property (including literary rights) is uncertain. If a repository's goal is to obtain unrestricted title to all acquisitions, the policy may prohibit accepting accessions on deposit. For those institutions that accept deposits, the policy should state the general conditions of deposit including its termination. Generally, the policy should prohibit unreasonable restrictions on access; allow clearly stated restrictions of limited duration; and require restrictions to be imposed by the donor or the repository when necessary to protect individual privacy.[8] The policy should also prohibit donations that impose unreasonable processing, special housing or other unwarranted requirements for the administration of the collection. Those institutions that require, as a condition of acceptance, major individual or corporate donors to defray the cost of processing, servicing, and preserving their collections, need to spell out this condition.

Conditions governing retention. Few, if any acquisitions, are retained in their entirety. As a general rule, the policy should permit the archives to dispose of those segments and/or items that are extraneous or otherwise unsuitable for retention. The policy should stipulate that the repository and the donor agree in advance regarding how unwanted material will be treated. Usually unwanted material will be separated from the collection and either transferred to an institution's library or museum, sold, returned to the donor, or destroyed.

The prudent acquisition policy will authorize the repository at some future time to transfer the information in the collection to a microform or other format and dispose of the original records. Some policies go further and state that acceptance is not a commitment by the repository to retain the accession in perpetuity.

Exclusions. The policy should state the types of material the repository will not accept. For example, many archives will not accept artifacts or other three-dimensional objects. Others exclude printed materials such as collections of newspaper clippings

---

[8] For details on deposit and loan agreements, and on access restrictions, see Chapter 9.

Figure 3-2 Collection Policy of the State Historical Society of Wisconsin

---

Field of Religion

10.1 *Collection Analysis Summary.* The Society's collection of religious manuscripts is large, containing extensive information about certain aspects of religious activity in Wisconsin. Records from individual churches document institutional history and sacramental activity for many traditional mainline Protestant denominations. Conference and statewide association records document collective denominational activity and stands on particular issues. Diaries, journals and recollections detail the observations and work of 19th century Protestant missionaries who traveled throughout Wisconsin. However, this documentation is narrowly focused, excluding almost entirely Catholics, evangelicals, minorities, and many non-traditional denominations. Existing records also contain little substantive information about church participation in social issues, political affairs, and individual or family welfare programs. Library resources are also extensive, including hundreds of individual church histories, journals, proceedings and newsletters of statewide or regional religious organizations, and secondary materials dealing with denominational history. Public records include the exhaustive Works Progress Administration church records inventory, which contains general information on several thousand Wisconsin churches and other religious organizations. Other Wisconsin college and religious archives also hold extensive religious documentation. Notable among these are St. Francis Seminary, Northwestern College in Watertown, and Marquette University, whose large collections of records documents Catholic missionary activity in Wisconsin. The University of Wisconsin System campus archives hold records documenting student religious organizations and activities. Finally, several major denominational archives located in other states have extensive holdings relating to Wisconsin.

10.2 The Society encourages religious organizations to establish their own archives, and to make their archival records available to researchers. The Society provides advice and assistance to churches and religious organizations considering the establishment of in-house archives.

10.3 The Society may act as the repository of last resort by accepting important religious manuscripts that otherwise might be destroyed.

10.4 The Society solicits religious records that document one of the following:
   a. the role of a church or religious group in the secular community
   b. the involvement of a religious group in social action and the non-sectarian world
      (*Related Subject:* 13.4)
   c. the role of a religious group within an ethnic community
   d. non-traditional or non-denominational religious groups

10.5 The Society accepts a representative sample of church records, private papers of religious leaders, and records pertaining to Wisconsin religious organizations.

10.6 Church records accepted for donation should meet one of the following guidelines:
   a. records from a denomination or group not adequately documented in Society holdings
   b. additions to an existing Society or ARC collection
   c. records not duplicated in denominational archives

---

or records written in particular foreign languages. There also are exclusions based on provenance. Learning from experience, some archival agencies will not serve as the repository "for large, ongoing commercial, non-profit or professional organizations capable of supporting their own archival programs." In exceptional cases when such records become endangered, the policy may provide that the archival

Figure 3-3   Collection Development Policy of the Florida State Archives (1987)

Congressional and Legislative Papers

The Congressional and Legislative Papers are a part of the Archives' Manuscript Collection. Because of the unique nature of these records, they are treated as a separate item in this policy. The Collection currently consists of the private official papers of members of the United States Congress and the Florida Legislature. Record types include correspondence, constituency files, personal committee papers, and issue files.

The Archives collects materials of state legislators and members of Congress based upon the individual's stature on the state, national, or international scene and the relationship with his/her constituency. These factors may include the following:

- The individual's position of power or influence within the legislative body, such as majority or minority leader or whip, caucus leader, or committee chairmanship.
- The period of service on a particular committee or subcommittee, especially one of importance in relationship to the issues of the day.
- The participation of the individual on special committees or task forces or his/her level of influence in current issues and events important to public policy or to the operations of the legislative body.
- The individual's level of expertise in one or more subject areas of substantial import to state or national policy.
- The member's length of service, especially those who have attained high seniority.
- The geographical area represented by the individual, his/her relationship with constituency, and his/her identification with a particular political or social philosophy, interest group(s), or issue(s).

In addition, the Archives' selection of Congressional and Legislative Papers is based upon the content quality of the collection. The Archives places an emphasis on acquiring materials that reflect the following:

- A comprehensive view of the operations of the individual member's office and its interactions with the constituency, as evidenced by a full range of files and file types. Such file types may include departmental, committee, general/subject, legislative/bill, press/public relations, constituent services, issue/ constituent correspondence, and schedules/speeches.
- A substantial body of correspondence and/or background materials on topics in which the individual is known to have been interested and involved.
- Information that documents or emanates from the member's service on important committees, subcommittees, causes, task forces, or that pertains to issues connected with these bodies' spheres of action.
- Information that complements or enhances the Archives' other collection areas.

The Archives will use the criteria outlined in this policy to select, in whole or in part, Congressional and Legislative Papers and will consult the National Historical Publications and Records Commission's "Congressional Papers Conference Report: Policy Considerations, June 3, 1986" for additional appraisal criteria.

---

agency serve as a "repository of last resort."[9] Most repositories will not accept split collections except under the most extenuating circumstances and many repositories severely limit the purchase of collections. Some limit purchases to materials of un-

usual importance that augment existing holdings or to collections for which special funding is available. (See Figure 3-4.)

Making exceptions to the policy. Inevitably, situations will arise in which common sense will dictate an exception to the policy. In making provisions for exceptions, the prudent policy will require the sub-

[9] "Collection Development Policy for Wisconsin Manuscripts," 6.

Figure 3-4 Criteria for Refusing Manuscript Collections

Over time, collecting has become increasingly focused at The Arthur and Elizabeth Schlesinger Library on the History of Women in America. At present the following types of papers are ordinarily neither sought nor accepted:

1) papers of non-United States women whose sphere of activity was not in the United States;

2) papers from other regions that are of primarily local or regional interest, such as the papers of an individual or family particularly connected with a city or town not in the Boston area, or a state other than Massachusetts;

3) papers of women whose careers are primarily identified with an educational or other institution or organization that has its own archives; such individuals might include faculty, staff, trustees, etc.;

4) literary manuscripts or the manuscripts or proofs of any published works;

5) the papers of women whose primary identification is as authors of fiction, poetry, or children's literature; or actors, musicians, and others in the performing arts; or painters, sculptors, and others in the visual arts; unless the creator was particularly concerned with the status of herself as a woman and of other women in her field or in society in general;

6) scientific papers, corporate records, or other large bodies of technical materials on any subject that have no specific relevance to women or women's issues other than the fact that the author or collector of the material is a woman;

7) the papers of social welfare agencies and organizations, *unless* the organization serves primarily women and children and is in the Commonwealth of Massachusetts, *and* the papers are in imminent danger of destruction;

8) papers of government officials or political figures that belong in a public city, state, or national archives, or in a local or regional repository; and

9) artifacts or papers of primarily "ceremonial" interest: for example, letters of congratulation or condolence, and plaques (except as portions of larger collections).

The Library must consider carefully the acceptance of records of extant organizations, especially if the existing records are voluminous and the organization is likely to continue to generate large quantities of records in the foreseeable future.

Collection Development Policy, *The Arthur and Elizabeth Schlesinger Library on the History of Women in America*

mission of a report to the program director or the head of the institution setting forth the compelling justification for the exception. Easy exceptions render a policy virtually inoperative.

4. Cooperation with other institutions. When cooperation in acquisition development is part of the institutional mandate, the policy should spell out its nature and extent. Three of the more common policy considerations for interinstitutional cooperation are: **one,** referring donors with out-of-scope collections or segments of a collection already in archival custody elsewhere to a more appropriate repository; **two,** assisting records creators or custodians to take responsibility and care for their own

archival records when such sharing of obligations advances the repository's own acquisition goals; and, **three,** factoring into the repository's policy and priorities the acquisition mandates of other institutions with parallel or closely related acquisition programs. For example, the Wisconsin Music Archives at the University of Wisconsin is the primary state repository for music written by Wisconsin composers or published in the state. The State Historical Society's Collection Development Policy recognizes this primacy by relying on the Music Archives to document this facet of the arts and referring donors of such material to that repository.

Figure 3-5 Summary of the Collecting Policy of the Billy Graham Center Archives

The purpose of the archives is to collect, house, and make accessible the documents of Billy Graham and the Billy Graham Evangelistic Association (BGEA) and to build a collection of documents that accurately reflects nondenominational evangelical North American Protestant evangelism and missions efforts. This balanced collection will be especially useful as a resource for Christian workers and scholars. The fact that no other institution is building this kind of theme collection increases the importance of the archives' work. Just as Billy Graham has been at the center of evangelism for a generation, the archives, by building a selected collection of major, repesentative documents, should be at the center of practical research in evangelism and missions.

We reaffirm the collecting policy adopted for the archives by the board of the Billy Graham Center in May, 1977 and particularly emphasize the following points:

1. The documents of Billy Graham, the Billy Graham Evangelistic Association, and the people associated with his ministry are of special importance to collect and form the nucleus of the archives' holdings.

2. The records of other individuals and organizations (save for exceptions listed below) are collected only if they have a direct importance for the history of North American, Protestant, or nondenominational evangelism and missions.

3. The files of international meetings relevant to evangelism and missions, such as the Amsterdam '83 conference, may be collected, since no one nation has a claim on them.

4. Similarly, the files of the International Office of Evangelistic Organizations may be collected, but not the files of the national branches of the same organization (except for North American branches). Thus, for example, the archives could collect the files of the international office of Overseas Missionary Fellowship, but not the files of the British branch.

5. The archives may acquire microfilmed collections of documents that relate to missions or evangelism, but which are not necessarily North American, Protestant, or nondenominational. Thus, for example, it could acquire the microfilm of Baptist Missionary Society files offered by the Southern Baptist Historical Commission, microfilm that includes the letters of William Carey and Adoniram Judson.

6. When the archives acquires the records of existing organizations other than the BGEA, those organizations should be charged at least part of the cost for shipping, storage, and/or processing in return for the record management services the archives provides.

7. Acquisitions should be limited to whatever extent necessary to maintain adequate space and maintenance for all BGEA archives now and in the foreseeable future.

Approved by the Billy Graham Center Committee of the Wheaton College Board of Trustees, February 15, 1985.

5. Deaccessioning. One requirement of modern collection management is that the acquisition policy provide for the future deaccessioning of records, including entire collections. The policy should spell out the steps—legal and otherwise—in deaccessioning: whether by sale, transfer to a more appropriate repository, return to the original custodian or donor (or his heirs), or destruction. Disposition of records in a governmental or other in-house repository is often accomplished by the same mechanism and authority that approved the original accessioning of the records.[10]

---
[10] See Chapter 10 on reappraisal and deaccessioning.

Policy Approval, Revision, and Enforcement

To validate institutional goals and commitment, to give the policy authority, and to support its disciplined application, the document must be approved by the repository's governing body. The policy should be continuously revised. A good acquisition policy will change over time, for it is not static but rather a living document that is refined and modified to reflect growth and changing conditions. Unless there is a revision process, the policy will become fossilized very quickly. The Florida State Archives policy, for example, stipulates an annual review. A sunset provision in the policy is another way to insure periodic review.

The repository needs to enforce the policy. Too many policies are rendered impotent because the repository lacks a mechanism—such as an accessions review group (see Chapter 7)—to enforce the policy or because staff—for personal, political, or other reasons—fail to follow the policy in making acquisition decisions.

Summary

• The purpose of an acquisition policy is to discipline the selection process; to delineate not only what repositories will potentially accession but what they will not acquire.

• Conceptualization must precede collection. The selection process does not start at the bottom, with a consideration of a specific set of records, but at the top, with an understanding of what is to be documented and what documentation is sought. The tools of collection analysis and functional analysis promote this understanding.

• Many repositories need to redefine their acquisition mandate in light of changing internal and external conditions and bring it in line with available resources. An unrealistic mission statement renders the acquisition policy useless.

• The heart of the policy is the delineation of acquisition fields. Collecting institutions often define fields topically while institutional repositories find functional or provenance-based fields more appropriate.

• The acquisition policy is the *sine qua non* for cooperation among archival institutions. It allows repositories to share their selection goals with others and thus can help avoid conflict and foster cooperation in collecting.

• To be effective, acquisition policies must be continuously revised and rigorously enforced.

Selected Readings

Frank Boles, "Mix Two Parts Interest to One Part Information and Appraise Until Done: Understanding Contemporary Record Selection Processes," *American Archivist,* 50 (Summer 1987), 356–68.

Canadian Council of Archives, *Guidelines for Developing an Acquisition Policy* (March 1990), 8pp.

Judith E. Endelman, "Looking Backward to Plan for the Future: Collection Analysis for Manuscript Repositories," *American Archivist* 50 (Summer 1987), 340–55.

Susan Grigg, "A World of Repositories, a World of Records: Redefining the Scope of a National Subject Collection," *American Archivist* 48 (Summer 1985), 286–95.

David H. Hoober, "Manuscript Collections: Initial Procedures and Policies," American Association for State and Local History Technical Leaflet No. 131, *History News* 35 (October, 1980).

Faye Phillips, "Developing Collecting Policies for Manuscript Collections," *American Archivist* 47 (Winter 1984), 30–42.

Helen W. Samuels, *Varsity Letters: Documenting Modern Colleges and Universities* (Metuchen, N.J.: Scarecrow Press, Inc., and Society of American Archivists, 1992).

State Historical Society of Wisconsin, "Collection Development Policy for Wisconsin Manuscripts" (Madison, 1986), 14 pp. and Appendices. Available upon request.

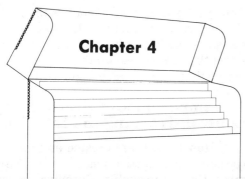

Chapter 4

Identifying Potential Accessions: The Role of Records Management in Archival Selection

With a repository's acquisition policy as a map to guide them, archivists are ready for the next step in the archival selection process: the identification and evaluation of those records of enduring value that will fulfill institutional goals.

Realizing the inadequacies—indeed, the perils—of having others make acquisition decisions for them, archivists have developed planned and active approaches to the record selection process. In general, archivists employ two basic methods to identify potential accessions. The first is a *systems* approach using the records management tools of inventory, analysis, and disposition scheduling to select archival records. The second, or *solicitation,* approach is used to identify, through an archival field collecting program, those historical records usually untouched by records management. The first approach is the basis of institutional or in-house repository acquisition programs. So fundamental is records management to the systems approach that the records management and archival programs are often integrated to form a combined records program. Solicitation is tailored to the needs of a collecting repository. Archivists need to be familiar with both methods. For example, while the archivist at Siwash University may receive most of his accessions through the records inventory and disposition scheduling process, earlier records alienated from university custody, papers of faculty members, and records of student activities and organizations usually have to be acquired through the solicitation process. Similarly, the staff of a collecting repository with organizational donors greatly benefit when they and their

clients use records management tools to designate archival records.

This chapter deals with the systems approach. It briefly examines the conceptual basis of records management. In the process, the chapter defines the record-life-cycle concept; those records management practices most important to archival appraisal and acquisition; and the archivist's role and responsibility in promoting these practices and in collaborating with records managers and others to achieve a common goal of creating and maintaining useful records.[1]

What Is Records Management?

Records management is the application of techniques designed to achieve efficiency and economy in the creation, utilization, and disposition of records. Its genesis was in efforts to cope with records spewed forth by New Deal programs of the 1930s and proliferating government agencies supporting America's World War II effort. Under the impetus of the burgeoning growth of records of the federal government, archivists at the National Archives expanded their responsibilities to manage records

---

[1] For a general introduction to records management, see Mary F. Robeck, Gerald F. Brown, and Wilmer O. Maedke *Information and Records Management,* 3rd edition (Encino, Calif.: Glencoe, 1987); and Betty R. Ricks and Kay F. Gow, *Information Resource Management: A Records Systems Approach,* 2nd edition (Cincinnati: South-Western Publishing Co., 1988).

Conducting an inventory of records in the second stage of the life cycle, active office use. (*Courtesy of the Massachusetts Archives*)

while they were still in current use and to plan for their disposition.

The Life Cycle Concept

Records management rests on the notion that records pass through four stages: (1) creation, (2) active administrative or office use, (3) semi- or inactive storage, and (4) final disposition, either by destruction or through preservation in an archives. During the first stage good records management promotes the production of needed documentation and prevents the creation of useless records. During the second phase it provides for the effective use of records through efficient filing systems that facilitate rapid information retrieval. When records are seldom needed for day-to-day administration, they enter the third phase. They are then segregated from active files, transferred from valuable office space, and placed in an intermediate storage facility called a records center, where storage and infrequent retrieval can be handled efficiently and economically. By the last phase of the cycle, when the records have generally lost their current administrative, fiscal, and legal usefulness, they are "a spent informational resource and a useless storage burden."[2] Most records are then destroyed, but a small remnant with usefulness for purposes for which they were not created—such as historical, genealogical, and other research uses—are transferred to archival custody.

---

[2] Bruce W. Dearstyne, *The Management of Local Government Records: A Guide for Local Officials* (Nashville: American Association for State and Local History, 1988), 39. This guide is a brief but excellent introduction for the novice.

Though the archivists' domain is the preservation of the historical record, they also need to participate in decisions made throughout the life cycle that will affect the quality, usefulness, and integrity of future archival accessions. (See Figure 4-1.)

The Importance of Pre-archival Control: Tracking the Life Cycle

How records are created and managed during the active and inactive stages of the cycle often determines the future quality of archival accessions. Decisions made about records, their file organization, access systems, and storage media can either facilitate or complicate the work of archival selection, preservation, and use. If records are logically organized from the beginning within a system that permits easy segregation of records of long-term value from those of transitory worth, the original records creator or custodian will have already completed much of the archivist's work.

To reap these benefits archivists must have a voice in the pre-archival management of current records. To know when to use this voice, archivists need a system to track records as they move through the life cycle, to know when archival intervention is necessary. Information obtained by tracking can be used to ensure the early identification of historically important records and their subsequent preservation. It can help expedite the flow of records through the stages of the life cycle. It can signal to the archivist what records need special handling, or timely accessioning. Tracking can help get records to the archives in a timely manner. To have an effective voice in pre-archival decisions about records, however, archivists must be plugged into the control system regulating records as they move through the life cycle. This connection will allow archivists to intervene promptly when it is appropriate. Pre-archival control is critical when dealing with technologically complex information systems. Decisions to insure their ultimate preservation and use as archival sources must be made when systems are set up; therefore archivists must be present at their creation.

The Process of Records Control: Inventory, Analysis, and Disposition

The life cycle concept is the framework for records control; inventorying and scheduling are the tools. Other important aspects of records management, such as file design and management and micrographics, help ensure the quality of the archival

Figure 4-1   Life Cycle of Records

Birth: Creation, receipt or computer generation of records and information.

Early in Life Cycle: Appraisal of values to determine retention requirements.

Legal?   Fiscal?   Historical?   Administrative?

Active Stage: Organization, handling and maintenance of information for immediate purposes.

Inactive or semiactive: Retirement to less costly storage space.

STATE RECORDS CENTER

Disposition: Either destruction of records or transfer to Archives for permanent preservation.

STATE ARCHIVES

R.I.P.

State of Wisconsin, *Filing Systems: Design and Implementation* (Madison, 1991)

Archivists' involvement in the early stages of a record's life cycle would interrupt the life cycle of pests (in this case, termites) that are detrimental to archival records (*Sharon B. Laist, Courtesy of The Ford Foundation*)

These archivists, on an inventory, appraisal, and "housecleaning" mission in Indonesia, know the importance of records management and pre-archival control. (*Sharon B. Laist, Courtesy of The Ford Foundation*)

record, but for the appraising archivist the most important records management tools are inventorying and scheduling.

Records Inventory. The inventory is a basic prerequisite for building a records management program. Its purpose is to gather data so managers can understand their institution's documentary system—can learn what records exist and are currently being created. The inventory provides the information necessary for decisions about the records program, especially when important actions occur in a record's life cycle. For the archivist, the inventory provides information about the records, their creator, functions, and the activities they document. This information is necessary to accurately appraise records.

The inventory primarily is designed to provide *series level* data about those aspects of a record that affect scheduling and disposition. The records series traditionally has been the basic unit of analysis for most aspects of the records work, whether scheduling and disposition, appraisal, arrangement and description, or reference, and it remains so today.

The Record Series: The Basic Unit of Analysis

Series are file units that are created, arranged, and maintained as a unit because they relate to a particular subject or function, result from the same activity, have the same form, or are related to each other in some other way. Simply put, they are records that belong together.

Bruce W. Dearstyne, *The Management of Local Government Records,* 1988

Specifically, a series level inventory should provide basic data about the composition, scope and content, and purpose of the record—who created the record, when and why. The information recorded should include the series title, the annual growth rate of the series, and the current total volume of accumulation. The inventory should also provide information on when and under what conditions the series is housed, either in active office space or inactive storage, who is the custodian of the series, how frequently the series is used, whether the information in the series has been transferred to another medium, whether the information is summarized or duplicated elsewhere, and whether there are indexes or other descriptive tools for the series. The inventory also should note the existence of any special laws or regulations governing series access, retention, and disposition.

A caveat about the record series as a unit of analysis: when archivists and records managers deal with technologically complex information systems, it is the system as an integrated whole and not its discrete components—source documents, databases, and output reports—that is the basic unit of analysis.[3]

Ideally, the inventory should be comprehensive and include all series of an entire program or administrative unit whether the series are active or inactive, on paper or in electronic data storage, or are text, aural, or visual materials. The inventory should be completed in a timely fashion, providing a snapshot of the institution's documentary resources. Inventory work should generally proceed from the highest offices down through the administrative hierarchy to capture organizational and reporting relationships. Within a unit, records personnel usually proceed retrospectively from the most current to the earliest records, from the more familiar to the less familiar. In some cases, information in more recent files may make older records more intelligible.

From the archivist's perspective the records inventory is first and foremost an intellectual inventory of the information landscape organized into manageable conceptual units called series and not a physical inventory of files and boxes.

Margaret Hedstrom, 1991

Record inventories are usually directed by the records manager, by the designated records officer of an administrative unit, or by the archivist. Office staff can carry out the actual examination and recording of information. Proper instruction and supervision will ensure the quality and uniformity of results. Many model forms are available that easily can be tailored to individual agency needs. Often a sample of the records themselves is attached to the inventory form to aid in record analysis and appraisal. (See Figure 4-2.)

Scheduling Records. The analysis of the data provided by the records inventory is used to prepare a records disposal schedule (also called a retention or retention and disposal schedule), the basic component of any records management system. The sched-

ule controls the records throughout their life cycle.[4] It governs where and how long the records will be retained and how they will be disposed of—the shredder or the archives—when the cycle is completed. The retention schedule converts an inventory from a one-time record snapshot to an ongoing control and disposal activity.

There are two basic types of schedules. One, the **specific schedule,** governs discrete series within a particular organizational unit such as Navistar International's divestiture records of the International Harvester Corporation's farm implement business. This kind of schedule is often referred to as an office-specific schedule. (See Figure 4-3.) The second type is the **general schedule,** a disposition plan that applies to common categories or applications of records, wherever they exist in a bureaucracy. For example, the general schedules drafted for the State University of New York's community colleges apply to such series as employee payroll and leave records, or personnel files, wherever they exist in the thirty institutions. (See Figure 4-4.)

For many facilitative or so-called "housekeeping" records, general schedules are an efficient, necessary way to dispose of ephemeral information. For more substantive documentation, these schedules are a coarse seine that cannot separate particular or exceptional information from the general or routine. Neither do general schedules provide for selecting a "view" or "slice" that is representative of the larger body of records. General schedules facilitate the destruction of vast quantities of routine records, but they make any partial or special selection virtually impossible. Despite this shortcoming, records administrators have come to use general schedules as their predominant disposition practice. Archivists, however, should use general schedules with care.

Scheduling and disposition are ongoing activities. Optimally, a record series should be scheduled and hence under archival control when it is created. The *Wisconsin Statutes,* for example, require state agencies to schedule records within one year of their creation. In the case of microforms, electronic records, and other fragile and/or ephemeral documentation, early scheduling is essential for archival preservation.

While some schedules provide a "one-time" authorization to dispose of a particular series of records covering a defined period of time, most schedules

---

[3] For information on the management of electronic records systems, see David Bearman, *Electronic Records Guidelines: A Manual for Policy Development and Implementation* (Pittsburgh: Archives & Museums Informatics, n.d. [1989]); and Margaret Hedstrom and Alan Kowlowitz, "Meeting the Challenges of Machine-Readable Records: A State Archives Perspective," *Reference Services Review* (1988), 31–40.

[4] See Carol Couture and Jean-Yves Rousseau, *The Life of a Document: A Global Approach to Archives and Records Management,* translated by David Homel (Montreal: Vehicule Press, 1987), 32 ff.

Figure 4-2 Records Inventory and Analysis Worksheet

INVENTORY AND ANALYSIS WORKSHEET

Department/Location_____ College of Letters and Science_____

_____ Dept. of Political Science_____

Contact Person/Telephone_____ W.C. Mona / x6979_____

Records Series Title_____ Law Studies - Major Program Files_____

(Other title by which series is known_____)

Span Dates_____1973 -_____Arrangement____Subject_____

Total Volume_____1.0 c.f._____Annual Accumulation____.20 c.f.____

Type of medium: _X_ paper ____ microfilm ____ machine readable ____ audio ____ other (specify)

Size of medium: _X_ letter ____ legal ____ disk ____ other (specify)

Yes	No	
_____	_X_	Is the records series covered by an existing RRDA? If yes, specify RRDA#_____
_____	_X_	Is the records series still being created?
_____	_X_	Is the records series confidential? If yes, specify statute(s)/citation(s)_____
		_____
_____	_X_	Is the records series duplicated? If yes, where? **[Explain on next page]**
		____ in the office ____ on campus ____ at the System level
_____	_X_	Is the records series indexed or summarized? If yes, specify_____

Indicate how often the records series is: <u>Daily</u>   <u>Monthly</u>   <u>Annually</u>   <u>Other</u> (Specify)

	Daily	Monthly	Annually	Other
Added to?	____	____	____	____
Referenced?	____	____	____	____

When is the records series referenced less than once per month? _____ Year/Month/Week (Ex: 3rd Year)

Detailed description of the records series: (Include types of documents [forms, reports, etc.] and the purposes and uses of the series.)

Series consists of materials involving the orgin and development of the Law Studies Major Program at this campus, including planning documents, authorizing documents, budget files, minutes of the Law Studies Program Committee, syllabi and informational material from law studies programs at other institutions, and the reports of consultants called in to evaluate the program.

Value of records series

_X_ Administrative value for __5__ years

_X_ Internal research value for __5__ years

_X_ Legal value for __7__ years

_X_ Audit value for __3__ years

_X_ Historical (permanent) value

Recommendation: Retain _5_ years in office of origin and ____ Destroy (or) _X_ Transfer to Archives
            for permanent retention

Using basic data elements found in a model worksheet, an archivist at the University of Wisconsin-Milwaukee designed this form to meet local needs as well as the requirements for completing the State's records retention/disposal authorization schedule (See Figure 4-3).

Figure 4-3   Office Specific Records Retention and Disposition Schedule

RECORDS RETENTION/DISPOSITION AUTHORIZATION   STATE OF WISCONSIN

INSTRUCTIONS
- Refer to separate, detailed instructions for completing this form.
- Shaded areas to be completed by Agency Records Officer. If you have any questions regarding completion of RDA, contact the Agency Records Officer.
- In accordance with s.16.61, Wis. Statutes, this form must be completed, approved by the Agency and the Public Records and Forms Board within one year of creation of the records series and prior to disposition of any public record.
- Forward to the Agency Records Officer for review and submission to the Public Records and Forms Board. A sample of the records series should be attached whenever possible.

RETENTION/DISPOSITION AUTHORIZATION (RDA #)		
Agency # 285 B	Sequential # 0 0 0 8 4	Suffix
Division # B48	Subdivision # (Optional) 6800	

Agency Name	Type of Request
University of Wisconsin - Milwaukee Campus	[X] New [ ] Amendment

Division Name	Subdivision Name	Old RDA System # (8 digits)
College of Letters and Scinece	Dept. of Political Science	

Records Series Title	Subject Code
Law Studies - Major Program Files	

Record Series Life Cycle Dates			Type of Medium
Year Created 1973	Year Discontinued	Year of Final Disposition	[X] Paper [ ] Microfilm [ ] Machine Readable [ ] Audio Recording [ ] Other (Specify):

Retention/Disposition

Retain: (RETENTION)

Years 5	Months	Weeks

After: (ACTION)
- [ ] Closed/terminated/death
- [ ] Superseded
- [ ] Microfilmed
- [ ] Entered in data system
- [ ] Federal audit
- [ ] State audit

After: (DISPOSITION)
- [ ] Destroy
- [ ] Destroy (confidential)
- [ ] Transfer-State Historical Society
- [X] Transfer-UW Archives with authority to weed
- [ ] Retain permanently

Provided: (CONDITION)
- [ ] Closed/terminated/death
- [ ] Superseded
- [ ] Microfilmed
- [ ] Entered into data system
- [ ] Federal audit
- [ ] State audit

Records Series Description

Series consists of materials involving the origin and development of the Law Studies Major Program at this campus, including planning documents, authorizing documents, budget files, minutes of the law studies program committee, syllabi and informational material from law studies programs at other institutions, and the reports of consultants called in to evaluate the program.

Filing Arrangement (Check all appropriate categories)

[ ] Alphabetic [ ] Numeric [ ] Chronologic [ ] Geographic [X] Subject [ ] Disarranged

Estimated Annual Accumulation	Is the Records Series Confidential?
.20 Cubic Feet	[X] No [ ] Yes — Specify Statute/Code:

AGENCY APPROVAL SIGNATURES

Agency (Optional)	Date	Agency Records Officer	Date
Allan Kovan - Univ. Archivist	2/20/88	Paul W. Rediske Director of Internal Audit	4/13/88

PUBLIC RECORDS & FORMS BOARD APPROVAL SIGNATURES - Contingent on restrictions on record destruction contained in s.19.35(5), Wis. Stats., (Open Records Law), and that no records be destroyed if litigation involving these records has commenced.

State Archivist	Date	Executive Secretary - PRFB	Date
F.G. Ham	8/1/88		

Figure 4-4   General Records Schedule for Community Colleges

General

ITEM NO.	DESCRIPTION OF RECORD	RETENTION

1. **Official minutes and meeting proceedings** (regardless of format) of Board of Trustees or committee thereof, and official faculty, student, or department committee meeting (including all records accepted as part of minutes):   PERMANENT

2. **Recording of voice conversations,** including audio tape, video tape, stenotype or stenographer's notebook, and also including verbatim minutes used to produce official minutes and hearing proceedings, report, or other record

   (a.) Recording of public meeting of Board of Trustees or committee thereof and official faculty, student, or department committee meeting: 4 months after transcription and/or approval of minutes or hearing proceedings

   NOTE: Audio and video tapes of public hearings or meetings at which significant matters are discussed may have continuing value for historical or other research. SARA suggests that community colleges retain these tapes permanently.

   (b.) Recording *other than* of public meeting: 0 after no longer needed

3. **Agenda** for meeting of Board of Trustees or committee thereof, and official faculty, student, or department meeting: 1 year

4. **Legal opinion or directive** rendered by local sponsor Board of Trustees: PERMANENT

5. **Resolution, rule, regulation, proclamation, or court order:**   PERMANENT

6. **Legal agreement,** including contract, lease, and release involving community college, Board of Trustees, or Student-Faculty Association (day care, book store, food service):   6 years after expiration or termination

7. **Signature card,** or equivalent record, showing signature of individual legally authorized to sign in specific transaction: 6 years after authorization expires or is withdrawn

8. **Proof of publication or posting,** or certification thereof: 6 years

9. **Manual of procedures,** or policies and standards: PERMANENT

10. **Correspondence,** and supporting documentation maintained in a subject file, generated or received, *except* correspondence that is part of a case file or other record series listed elsewhere on this Schedule

    (a.) Documenting significant policy or decision making: PERMANENT

    NOTE: Significant correspondence is often maintained by the President. See item no. 1 under PRESIDENT.

    (b.) Containing legal, fiscal, or administrative information: 6 years

    (c.) Of *no* fiscal, legal or administrative value (including letters of transmittal, invitations, and cover letters):   1 year

Records Retention and Disposition Schedule CC-1 For Use by Public Community Colleges (Albany, N.Y.: New York State Archives and Records Administration, 1988).

are "continuing" or "ongoing" and govern records disposition until revoked. Because the character of a record series or appraisal judgments may change over time, retention and disposal schedules should be reviewed periodically. Wisconsin law, for example, requires that all schedules be reviewed and reauthorized after ten years.

Schedules should apply to all types of documents and media and should cover all records within an administrative unit. Schedules are usually prepared by either records management staff or the records officer in an administrative unit. Many organizations require that records retention schedules be reviewed by an archival authority before they are approved. Thus, receipt by the archivist of disposal schedules for review in many cases triggers the appraisal process, and the archivist's decision is written into the schedule. Because they provide authority either to destroy records or to transfer them to an archival authority, these schedules are also called records disposal authorizations or rules. In the public sector the schedules are usually approved by a records review board or commission whose actions make these schedules a legal document. Whether the agency is public or private, schedules should be approved at the highest administrative level to reinforce the importance and authority of disposition mandates.

The following are some caveats on the scheduling of records:

• Record schedules are not necessarily self-enforcing. To assure that records scheduled for transfer to the repository arrive in a timely fashion—or at all—the archivist must closely monitor disposal schedules and enforce compliance with their provisions. In extreme cases, the archivist may have to requisition records unduly retained in a custodial office.

• In many organizations, the high-level records on policy formulation and executive direction too often escape the scheduling process. In this case, the archivist must either see that the records of archival value are scheduled or otherwise negotiate for their eventual transfer to the archives. The effectiveness of record scheduling is a function of comprehensiveness and compliance.[5]

---

[5] A study of the Public Archives of Canada's Federal Archives Division noted that well over 30 percent of its records was acquired by means outside the normal application of records schedules. See Bryan Corbett and Eldon Frost, "The Acquisition of Federal Government Records; A Report on Records Management and Archival Practices," *Archivaria* 17 (Winter 1983–84), 203.

Other Archival Uses of Inventory and Scheduling Information. Much of the information and analysis which comes from the inventory and scheduling process will be of value to archivists in managing those records transferred to their custody. A well-designed inventory and/or retention schedule will provide archivists with much of the information needed to control the records. The information facilitates initial accessioning, arrangement, description, and use. In effect, the inventory or disposal schedule is the beginning of the archival descriptive process. Another important by-product of the scheduling process is improved archival reference service. The process provides the archivist with a comprehensive listing of records and their custodians wherever they may be held, and tells reference archivists about records not yet accessioned by a repository. Inventory and scheduling data also are essential for management planning. This information, especially in an automated form, can tell the archivist the number and volume of accessions scheduled to come to the repository in any period of time, allowing the archivist to plan for the processing, servicing, and, above all, the storage of future accessions.

Other Components of a Records Management Program

Among the several other program components needed for efficient records administration, two merit the archival appraiser's special attention. These are file management and micrographics.

File Management. Appropriate file structure can segregate records of long-term value from those of transitory use and thus facilitate appraisal and other archival processes. As a result of carefully considered file design and maintenance, the archivist can accession records with most of the weeding or purging already completed. When appraising records, the archivist should carefully examine file structure and, where necessary or possible, suggest changes to the records custodian that will facilitate the appraisal of future accessions.

Micrographics. To archivists, one of records management's most alluring tools is micrographics. When original records are microfilmed according to established standards, the archivist can then accession records that are usually well-organized in a compact, long-lasting, and easily duplicated format. But, to assure these advantages, the archivist must be sure that the source documents are well-organized and described in a manner that will facilitate retrieval; that film stock, microfilming, and film pro-

Micrographic decisions are important to the records creator, the archivist, and the researcher. (*Courtesy of Melanie A. Amble*)

cessing conforms to American National Standards Institute standards; and that the master negative is stored in a controlled and protected environment. Many archivists have faced the difficult choice of accessioning either bulky records or substandard microfilm when timely archival intervention might have resulted in a microfilm product that better served the needs of both the records creator and the archivist.[6]

The Importance of an Archives-Records Management Alliance

Archivists who are uninformed about basic records management functions and isolated from records management operations weaken their program for selecting records. The scope of archival intervention throughout the life cycle requires close collaboration of archivists with records managers and other information specialists. Many governmental, university, and corporate archives have therefore integrated archival and records management functions into a combined program.

Other institutional archives programs, however, operate independently of the agency's records management program. Many archives are handicapped in assembling an institution's records because they lack any records management program at all. Either situation can complicate and frustrate

the work of archival selection. Therefore, in the first situation, the archivist must develop an effective working relationship with the records management staff. In the second situation, the archivist may find it necessary to initiate a basic inventory, analysis, and disposition program or instruct others on how to carry out these activities.

To develop a partnership with records managers, archivists must become knowledgeable about those records management functions that affect the quality and condition of future archival accessions. Archivists need to see records managers as partners, not merely useful technicians, in the work of identifying, selecting, and preserving the archival record. This collaboration allows archivists, as Karen Paul points out, to "rationalize and economize archival and information services within a larger institutional structure."[7] Together, archivists and records managers need to promote broad record program objectives regarding the creation, maintenance, and preservation of useful documentation.

Modern information technology is making collaboration imperative, for the more sophisticated the technology that produced the records, the closer the archivist must work with all those who deal with the records. This is particularly true of information in electronic format. As Margaret Hedstrom noted, where archivists and records managers must plan for the destruction of traditional paper records, with electronic records they must plan for their preservation. Doing nothing ensures the record's obsolescence and uselessness. In part, this is the result of the decentralization of electronic information processing. Without established data management and retention guidelines, the record creator becomes an information manager deciding what information to retain and destroy.[8]

At times the alliance between archivists and records management has been strained. Records management personnel are concerned with the efficient maintenance and disposition of records, while archivists must focus on the record's long-term research value before making judgments about economy. In reality, collaboration provides for a systems of checks and balances in which the archivist's acquisitive proclivities and the records manager's con-

---

[6] A brief but comprehensive listing of standards for preparing, filming, and storing archival quality microforms is in Dearstyne, *The Management of Local Government Records*, 88–90. A standard work on micrographics is Daniel M. Costigan, *Micrographics Systems*, 2nd ed. (Silver Spring, Md.: National Micrographics Association, 1980).

[7] Karen Dawley Paul, "Archivists and Records Management," in James G. Bradsher (ed.), *Managing Archives and Archival Institutions* (Chicago: University of Chicago Press, 1988), 36.

[8] Hedstrom and Kowlowitz, "Meeting the Challenges of Machine-Readable Records," 38.

Archivists load records for transfer to an intermediate storage center (the third stage in the record life cycle) in an incremental records management program that now includes records storage and retrieval services. (*Courtesy of the University of Wisconsin Archives*)

cern for short-run operational cost-effectiveness are balanced.[9]

The Archivist as Records Manager: An Incremental Approach to Implementing a Basic Records Management Program

So vital is basic records management to the selection of institutional records that archivists need to promote its adoption in institutions where it does not exist. First, they need to educate institutional decision-makers about a records management program's value. An assessment report on current record-keeping practices and potential benefits of a program to the institution is very useful. Second, archivists may have to invest their own resources. Many records programs have begun as ad hoc attempts to identify and schedule the institution's more important records.

If a full-scale records program is not feasible, archivists should consider an incremental or "project-oriented strategy." This strategy focuses on areas of highest priority: for example, inventorying and

scheduling organizational units with the most records or with endangered records. Some archivists suggest giving attention to those offices with the highest turnover in top personnel whether they be athletic coaches or politicians. There are many variations on this theme: one example is implementing a file design program for an office where archivally important records are particularly difficult to appraise due to filing chaos.[10]

The records management connection is not just for the in-house archival program. Many corporate organizations transfer their records to "compliant or solicitous" repositories, to use Richard Berner's words. The extent to which these records benefit from good file management and systematic scheduling and disposition will both facilitate appraisal and provide more comprehensive and complete documentation.[11]

Summary

The records management approach to records selection has many advantages for the archivist. It can

- facilitate the early identification and appraisal of records by providing the archives with detailed information about the total documentation of an agency.
- provide a control system to ensure archivists receive records, especially those with special preservation requirements, on a timely and regular basis rather than passively waiting for unplanned transfers.
- facilitate the separation of the valuable from the valueless and prevent the archives from becoming a dumping ground for unwanted records.
- stop the build-up of inactive records that lead to periodic and sometimes ill-conducted house cleanings by establishing an orderly and continuing flow of records to the archives.
- provide easy access to the records and reduce costs of servicing the records.
- give the archivist data necessary for planning staff, space, and other needs by providing information on future accessions, their form and volume, and the date of transfer.

---

[9] See Frank B. Evans, "Archivists and Records Managers: Variations on a Theme," *American Archivist* 30 (January 1967), 45–58; and Robert L. Sanders, "Archivists and Records Managers: Another Marriage in Trouble?" *ARMA Records Management Quarterly* (April 1989), 12–20.

[10] The incremental approach to records management is treated in detail in John Dojka and Sheila Conneen, "Records Management as an Appraisal Tool in College and University Archives," in Nancy E. Peace (ed.), *Archival Choices: Managing the Historical Records in an Age of Abundance* (Lexington, Mass: D.C. Heath, 1984), 19–40.

[11] Richard C. Berner, *Archival Theory and Practice in the United States: A Historical Analysis* (Seattle: University of Washington Press, 1983), 179–80.

• facilitate basic archival functions of arrangement, description, reference, and preservation.

Records management is a tool, not a panacea.

To assure the transfer of records appraised and scheduled for archival preservation, the archivist must closely monitor disposition schedules for compliance. The archivist must also make sure that records documenting high-level policy formulation and executive direction do not slip through the scheduling net or, if they do, that some other process is in place to assure their appraisal and possible retention.

By collaborating with records managers, archivists can more effectively deal with problems of compliance and comprehensiveness. In the electronic information age, it is also imperative that archivists and records managers develop close collaboration with other information management professionals, that they be intimately involved in decisions affecting the maintenance and disposition of information resources, and that they promote the development and implementation of data management and retention guidelines.

Selected Readings

Carol Couture and Jean-Yves Rousseau, *The Life of a Document: A Global Approach to Archives and Records Management*. Translated by David Homel (Montreal: Vehicle Press, 1987), 51–154.

Bruce W. Dearstyne, *The Management of Local Government Records: A Guide for Local Officials* (Nashville: American Association for State and Local History, 1988).

John Dojka and Sheila Conneen, "Records Management as an Appraisal Tool in College and University Archives," in Nancy E. Peace (ed.), *Archival Choices: Managing the Historical Record in an Age of Abundance* (Lexington, Mass.: D.C. Heath, 1984), 19–40.

Karen Dawley Paul, "Archivists and Records Management," in James G. Bradsher (ed.), *Managing Archives and Archival Institutions* (Chicago: University of Chicago Press, 1988), 34–52.

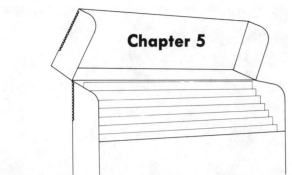

Chapter 5

Identifying Potential Accessions: The Logistics of an Archival Collecting Program

Identifying and accessioning archival records through the systematic management of current records is a comparatively recent approach that still leaves much of the archival landscape untouched. The records kept by individuals and families, often called personal papers, as well as those of most organizations—social, religious, professional, cultural, or business—remain outside the systems approach. To identify, evaluate, and bring these records into repository custody, archivists employ a method called field collecting.

Field collecting has a venerable history in this country. Throughout most of the nineteenth and well into the twentieth century, this method of acquisition was the primary means of saving the nation's archival treasures. Field collecting was the preserve of both institutional collectors, such as the Library of Congress, and private collectors—whether would-be historians gathering their own research material or amateur scholars with a passion for acquisition in their area of expertise. This approach relied on the enterprise, interest, instinct, inspiration—and often money—of individuals, not on some grand and methodical collecting design.[1]

This somewhat disorderly process also fostered competition and conflict among collecting institutions, and happenstance and fragmentation in collec-

tion building. Today, largely because of documentary overabundance, field collecting has become more orderly and organized and less competitive. By fashioning well-focused and achievable collecting policies and paying greater attention to planned acquisition, the better archival collecting agencies have developed systematic and efficient field collecting programs to identify potential collections, contact their custodians, evaluate the material's worth, and negotiate for its acquisition.

The major components of such a program are (1) staffing, (2) developing "leads" to potential archival collections and their owners or custodians, (3) tracking the pursuit of these "leads," (4) contacting the donor and appraising the records, and (5) negotiating for the transfer of the records to archival custody. Other program considerations—acquisition by purchase, informational material for prospective donors, and continuing donor support for repository programs—are discussed at the conclusion of the chapter.

Staffing

Many staffing patterns exist. A few larger agencies have one or more persons assigned full-time to the field collecting program. In smaller repositories, the chief archivist or another staff member assumes responsibility for collecting along with other duties. Field work also may be shared among several staff members. Some institutions have integrated collection development with collection management and have assigned subject specialists responsibility for both acquisition and processing, allowing for

[1] For a brief discussion of the antecedents of modern field collecting, see Donald R. McNeil (ed.), *The American Collector* (Madison: State Historical Society of Wisconsin, 1955); and Lucile M. Kane, "Manuscript Collecting," in William B. Hesseltine and Donald R. McNeil (eds.), *In Support of Clio: Essays in Memory of Herbert A. Kellar* (Madison: State Historical Society of Wisconsin, 1958), 29–48.

greater appraisal expertise. In an institution that also has an historical library, the archival field staff often is assigned some of the library collection development responsibilities.

Whatever the staffing arrangements, there are some basic qualifications for field collecting. Just as the institutional archivist must have a thorough understanding of the agency's history and functions, so archival solicitors must have a similar knowledge of historical and current developments in their repository's area of specialization and maintain this expertise by reading the recent literature in that field. Field agents must excel at historical detective work. They must have a thorough knowledge of the institution's holding and collecting focus. Field representatives should possess the ability to make sound, on-the-spot appraisals of the record's historical value. Finally, they must negotiate with the utmost integrity. The best field agents have the nose of a bloodhound, the persistence of a Fuller Brush salesman, and the tact of a diplomat. Above all, they enjoy the thrill of the chase.

There is nothing like having a *good repository* and *keeping a good look out,* not waiting at home for things to fall in the lap, but prowling about like a wolf for the prey.

Jeremy Belknap, founder of the Massachusetts Historical Society, to Ebenezer Hazard, 1795.

Developing Leads

Lacking the institutional archivist's comprehensive records inventory to provide an overview of available documentation, the collecting archivist must develop information or leads about the custodian, content, and location of potential accessions. In gathering this information, the archivist must employ both method and imagination. The methods are: record surveys; reviews of current literature; information from previous donors, researchers, repository holdings, obituaries; and broadcast techniques.

Records Surveys. Archivists or records managers in an institutional setting inventory to determine the universe of agency or departmental records. Archivists from collecting repositories use surveys to determine a universe of material documenting an activity, subject, area, or locale.[2] While

---

[2] See John A. Fleckner, *Archives & Manuscripts: Surveys* (Chicago: Society of American Archivists, 1977).

On-site survey by an archivist from a collecting repository. (*Balch Institute for Ethnic Studies, Philadelphia*)

some surveys have been massive, national undertakings—such as the Works Progress Administration's Historical Records Survey under the New Deal—most, like the 1982 National Historical Publications and Records Commission-sponsored survey of records documenting the Polish-American community in Milwaukee, are local, regional, and/or topical in scope. Surveys are seldom ongoing activities but rather are part of special projects to locate specific documentation. They are expensive and unless there is timely follow-up the collected data quickly diminish in value.

Current Literature. The current literature in the area of institutional acquisition interests can be a prolific source of leads. Current literature comes from a variety of sources. To suggest a few: newspapers from the *The New York Times* to the Wauzeka (Wis.) *Kickapoo Papoose;* newsletters of volunteer organizations, corporate enterprises, and trade organizations; and, of course, scholarly studies.

Previous Donors. Established donors are knowledgeable about and often acquainted with important persons or organizations in their field. Donors are an excellent source for leads, particularly to collections related to their own. One example of a donor's importance is the State Historical Society of Wisconsin's acquisition of the papers of the Hollywood Ten. The Ten were a group of screenwriters who were blacklisted by the motion picture establishment in the late 1940s and early 1950s for refusing to testify about their alleged leftist connections before the House Un-American Activities Committee. Using information from the initial donor, Dalton Trumbo, as a lead to the others, the repository eventually received the papers of seven of the Ten along with the records of the Hollywood Democratic Committee which provided the Ten legal and other support. In this instance, the donor not only provided lead information but also personal entree to prospective donors.

The Donor's Collection. As a corollary, the archivist may also find the donor's records a fruitful source of leads. The wise archivist will be alert to information in the records about the interconnection between the collection's primary creator, whether personal or corporate, and related colleagues and organizations. In this regard, the archivists that process the records are central to the collecting program.

Researchers. Researchers using the repository's holdings are a source of potential leads, for they often know about collections in private hands that are related to their research. Two researchers working on late nineteenth-century foreign trade and diplomacy, for example, were instrumental in the State Historical Society of Wisconsin's accessioning the records of the Singer Manufacturing Company. Like donors, researchers often provide entree as well as leads, for they may have already tracked down and used the prospective donor's records. They may also suggest prime actors who should be contacted to learn if they have records.

Friends of the Institution. Important collections often belong to persons with a deep loyalty to the archives' parent institution, such as a college or university, or who serve as friends of a cultural institution affiliated with the archives. These loyalties can lead to major acquisitions. For example, colleges often have first claim on the papers of their alumni. Members of governing boards or friends of the archives also can play an active role in providing entree to potential donors.

Obituaries. Though it may sound a bit ghoulish, some archivists regularly read personal or corporate obituaries to discover the demise of individuals and organizations whose activities were in the area of the institution's acquisitions policy. However, important people and organizations often make disposition decisions long before they die. Even when they do not, the archivist reading an obituary may be too late, for the heirs, corporate or personal, often clean house quickly.

Broadcast Techniques. Some archival agencies use devices such as mass mailings to targeted audiences, exhibits at special events, and newspaper press releases, particularly about new accessions, to locate potential accessions. These methods raise people's consciousness about the importance of records preservation, but they often produce few leads.[3] One exception to this generalization is the University of Wisconsin-LaCrosse, which periodically published a mystery photograph from its regional history collection in the city's newspaper. The public's interest in identifying the photograph increased the donation of photographs to the collection. By and large, however, these broadcast techniques are too impersonal for archival field collecting.

Tracking Potential Collections

The life cycle concept is not limited to the records of large bureaucratic organizations. The papers of a writer, social action groups, or the local PTA follow the same cycle, though usually in a less controlled and organized way. Tracking these records is important for collecting agencies, for the materials tend to be more fragile and ephemeral than corporate records and more subject to personal whim and indifference.

To track leads, a collecting repository must have an information management system that provides accurate, accessible, and timely information about potential collections and the status of negotiations with prospective donors. The acquisition process often drags on and may even be suspended temporarily. To resume the process, the archivist needs a complete record of past negotiations. Further, adequate and accurate information can minimize misunderstandings that often arise in negotiations over family and personal papers. Most field collecting operations use an uncomplicated information system that has but two components: the donor **lead file** and the donor **case file.**

---

[3] Steve Gurr, "Collecting for Clio: The Perspective of an Historian/Archivist," *Georgia Archive* 3:1 (Winter 1975), 32.

The Lead File. For a collecting repository, the lead file serves much the same purpose as the retention and disposition schedule. It is used to record information about potential accessions and to track contacts and negotiations with their owners. The lead record, usually a sheet in a manual file or a single record in a database, should include basic information such as the name, address, and telephone number of the prospective donor, current custodian of the records, or other persons to be contacted; the source of the lead; the main functions or activities of the record creator, whether an individual or corporate body; and what records the donor is supposed to have relating to these functions or activities. Much of this information is tentative and incomplete, and, before an initial contact is made, the archivist needs to do research to verify and amplify initial lead file data. (See Figures 5-1 and 5-2.)

Most repository lead files are organized alphabetically by the name of the records' creator, current custodian, or owner. Where field activity is organized on a geographic basis, such as state, region, county, or city, some repositories supplement the name file with a second file organized by geographic location to facilitate more systematic field operations. Many donor leads turn out to be dead ends. To prevent the buildup of a file of such leads, new leads should be investigated as soon as possible.

If the lead proves viable, the record will be updated as needed to provide a complete record of all transactions pertaining to the potential acquisition including donor contacts by correspondence, telephone, and in person; actions to be taken and in what time frame; donor requests for information; and receipt of accession(s). The lead file becomes a brief history—a docket or minute—of negotiations with the donor.

Case File. The information system's second element is a case file created for each active lead and containing the actual documentation of contacts and negotiations for a particular acquisition. The case file may include correspondence with the prospective donor; newspaper and other notices about the collection or its creator; notes on provenance, content, and organization of the collection; information on whether parts of the collection were donated elsewhere, destroyed, or otherwise missing; a copy of the deed of gift or other legal documents affecting collection transfer and access; and any other material relating to the potential accession.

The case file remains active until the lead is discontinued or the records are accessioned into archival custody. At the latter point, some repositories convert the donor case file, along with lead file information, into a collection accession file where it will be needed by the archivists arranging and describing the records.

In addition to these two basic files, many archives maintain a tickler file and a series of field reports.

Tickler File. Many archivists use a tickler file to remind staff when certain actions need to be taken, such as contacting the donor on the next field trip, having legal counsel examine the transfer instrument, or arranging for packing and shipping. Tickler files are almost always arranged chronologically.

Field Reports. This report, described in more detail below, contains a record of actions resulting from field contact with the potential donor, which also will be noted on the lead card.

Just as archivists are beginning to use automated systems to track and control scheduled records, archival collecting programs have begun to utilize automation in controlling information about prospective donors. If information is properly organized, an automated system can present data in a variety of ways, such as by topic or activity, geographic area, status of negotiations, pending actions, or type of record. An automated system also facilitates management analysis of collecting activities.

Contacting the Potential Donor

Although an archivist's unannounced knock on the door has been the first entree to acquiring some large and important collections, generally there is a better protocol. How the archivist contacts the donor, of course, depends on many factors—the donor, the geographic location, the person making the contact, and the significance of the collection.

The first step in contacting prospective donors is for archivists to introduce themselves and the repository. Unless the archivist has some special entree, such as a mutual friend, the initial introduction is accomplished through a letter stating the archivist's interest in both the materials and verifying the accuracy of the lead. Usually the letter also should inform the person how the archivist was led to make the contact, such as the suggestion of a current donor who is also an acquaintance of the person. Accompanying the letter should be a brochure describing the archives collecting program. Though an initial letter is a necessary first step, the probability is high that the repository will not receive a response much less an accession. In the initial letter, therefore, the

Figure 5-1   Donor Lead/Contact File Record

Archives of Labor and Urban Affairs Collections
Lead/Contacts

Date Entered   2-8-82

Collection Title   Jacobs, Harrison

Prospective Donor   Jacobs, Barbara   **Home phone**   313-571-3042

Street Address   1621 Dort Blvd.   **City**   Flint   **State**   MI   **Zip Code**   48202

Office Address   **Office phone**

Source of Information   Roger Brown, Former President UAW Local 599

Brief Biographical Sketch (include affiliations, reasons for Archives' interest, special notes)

Harrison Jacobs was born in Flint, Michigan in 1910. Attended University of Michigan 1928–30; Commonwealth College 1930–32. Active in auto industry. Helped organize autoworkers in Flint. Leadership role in Flint Sit Down Strike. Affiliated with Communist group in Flint; left UAW in 1941. U.S. Army. Died 1944. Widow—Barbara Jacobs. Has husband's papers and willing to give them to Archives, according to John Boyd, Flint UAW official.

(attach additional Biographical data)

Follow-up

Date	Visit Summary
2-7-82	Visited Mrs. Jacobs at home in Flint. Reviewed 10 boxes of records in garage. Diaries, correspondence, UAW newspapers, photographs. 2 boxes of records of Flint Vigilante organization. Stolen by Jacobs group during Flint Sit Down Strike. 3 boxes of records borrowed from Local Union leader. Jacobs had planned to write book about strike. Special problems: 1. Damaged records need attention. 2. Photos need identification. 3. Ownership of two groups of records need to be resolved. 4. Folder re: correspondence between Harrison Jacobs and father closed. Follow-up: 1. Collection will be processed by September 1, 1982. 2. Send guide to Mrs. Jacobs. 3. Send invitation to Mrs. Jacobs to visit Archives. 4. All duplicate records can be destroyed. 5. Copies of family photos returned to Mrs. Jacobs. 6. Prepare deed of gift, transferring literary rights to the Archives. 7. Mrs. Jacobs will try to locate additional files in summer college. 8. Contact in Fall 1981.
3-1-82	Deed of gift signed and returned to Archives.
8-16-82	Guide completed, sent to Mrs. Jacobs, along with photos.
9-16-82	Mrs. Jacobs and daughters visited Archives; gave leads to other collections.
4-6-89	Received 6 boxes of records from Mrs. Jacobs; to be added to original Jacobs Collection. All restrictions removed from Collections.

Figure 5-2 Donor Lead/Contact File Record Segments of an Automated Archival Information Management System

---

Johnston's Lodge and Outfitters

Screen 1: Donor Identification Segment

DONOR CODE:	796 *[computer generated ID number]*
FIRST NAME:	Mark
MIDDLE NAME:	William
LAST NAME:	Johnston
ORGANIZATION NAME:	Johnston's Lodge and Outfitters
STREET ADDRESS:	1345 Washburn Road
CITY:	Cable
STATE:	WI
ZIP CODE:	54701
COUNTRY:	USA
PHONE NUMBER:	(715) 834-7671
REVIEW CODE:	92/06 *[date for next review of lead]*
COUNTY CODE:	S5 *[used for trip planning and lead analysis]*
CROSS REFERENCES:	Jason Pringel
BIO SUMMARY:	Mark Johnston is the third generation of his family to operate the lodge and outfitters (established 1913) specializing in fishing and hunting trips in northern WI, MN, and Canada.

Screen 2: Donor Transaction Segment

DONOR CODE:	796
TRANSACTION:	1
TYPE OF CONTACT:	P *[phone call]*
DATE:	3/25/91
TEXT NOTE:	Mark Johnston called. Heard from Pringel SHSW interested in resort recs. He interested in donating. Has guest lists, finance recs, equip inventories, brochures back to begin 1913. I expressed interest in coll. promised to visit next time in area.
STAFF MEMBER:	CO *[initials of staff member making contact]*

****

DONOR CODE:	796
TRANSACTION:	2
TYPE OF CONTACT:	L *[letter]*
DATE:	3/29/91
TEXT NOTE:	CO to MJ: Appreciated your notifying us of coll. SHSW very interested in documenting resort business as part of tourism. Next time staff in area will schedule visit.
STAFF MEMBER:	CO

****

DONOR CODE:	796
TRANSACTION:	4
TYPE OF CONTACT:	V *[visit]*
DATE:	9/22/91
TEXT NOTE:	Very cordial meeting. Good set, although not complete in places. Full run guest books with addresses & annual photos dating to 1913. Finance, publicity, inventories, trip planning materials date from 1940. Bulk of coll. is canceled checks/receipts dating to 1925. Also has excellent family corr. dates 1890 to 1953. Willing donate guest books now, 1913–1960. MJ not ready donate other materials yet, wants time to review coll. for personal info. MJP said will call back next year.
STAFF MEMBER:	MJP

****

DONOR CODE:	796
TRANSACTION:	5
TYPE OF CONTACT:	T *[tickler]*
DATE:	6/1/92
TEXT NOTE:	Recontact re donation of additions.
STAFF MEMBER:	MJP

Screen 3: Bibliographic Record Segment

DONOR CODE:	796
GEOG. CLASS CODE:	4123S5 *[geographic identifier]*
SUBJECT CODE:	RA *[from NHPRC subject list]*
MAIN ENTRY:	Johnston Family
TITLE:	Papers
BEGINNING YEAR:	1913
ENDING YEAR:	1991
RESTRICTIONS:	
SUMMARY:	The collection consists of guest registers, photographs (1913–present), equipment inventories, publicity fliers, and trip planning materials (1940–present) documenting the operation of a family resort and outfitter founded in 1913 and specializing in hunting and fishing trips to northern Wisconsin, Minnesota and Canada. Also includes family correspondence discussing the business and family affairs (1913–present).
THESAURUS TERMS:	RLc *[from SHSW subject list]*

[Note: bibliographic record would be started at time of first contact and updated as negotiations progress.]

This system, based on a manual one in use since the later 1950s, is under development at The State Historical Society of Wisconsin.

archivist should inform potential donors they will be contacted in the next few weeks.

Psychologically, some people react to a request for their records as they would to one asking them to arrange for their own funeral. A field representative should understand this reaction and turn it to advantage, pointing out that the person's records and papers are, in fact, an affirmation of the importance of the person's life's work. If representatives have done their homework, this affirmation is genuine. When the donors are the heirs of the records' creator, the archivist can point out the importance of the papers as a lasting memorial to the deceased.

Many solicitors will not waste time with a second letter, but let their fingers do the walking. A telephone call is an appropriate second step. Though some donors, or their intermediaries, continue to put the archivist off, others often respond: "I've been meaning to answer your letter." Having made contact, the archivist should be able to verify the lead and determine whether or not it should be pursued. Occasionally, successful negotiations can be accomplished by correspondence and telephone, but most negotiations require personal contact. The willingness of a prospective donor to open discussions in person—to become a potential donor—is the third and often critical step.

I received a letter from Boston University asking me to consider making the BU library the repository of my . . . [papers]. "Your work is much admired here," the letter whispered seductively. It ended by urging me to "give the proposal for a Marcia Biederman Collection some thought". . . . The more I looked at the . . . letter, the more it began to resemble another piece of mail that arrived in the same delivery (MARCIA BIEDERMAN! YOU MAY ALREADY HAVE WON. . . .) I wondered if the same principle was at work in both.

Marcia Biederman, "From the Collection of . . . ," *1990 Writers' Yearbook*

Most donor contacts and subsequent negotiations are handled by the field archivist or other delegated members of the archives staff. There are, however, special situations when participation by someone outside the archival staff may be advantageous. This is particularly true for certain high-level contacts involving the prominent or the vain—a United States Senator, a corporate chief executive officer, a well-known writer, or a star of arts and entertainment. In these situations, entree and initial

contacts might be more effectively made by the parent institution's head, a member of the board of trustees, or another donor closely acquainted with the current prospect. John L. Lewis, the feisty and acerbic head of the United Mine Workers, was a case in point. He refused to acknowledge any communication from the archival director at West Virginia University, the repository seeking his papers. Only when he was approached jointly by the university president, the head of the Chesapeake and Ohio Railroad, and the CEO of one of America's largest coal companies, would he meet to discuss disposition of the John L. Lewis-UMW records. Walter Reuther, as head of the United Automobile Workers, assisted the director of Wayne State University's Archives of Labor and Urban Affairs in opening negotiations that resulted in the acquisition of the records of the Congress of Industrial Organizations and the United Farm Workers records and approximately fifty collections of personal papers. Archival field representatives should recognize those situations in which they need assistance and select the proper gauge armament to bring down the quarry.

The Field Trip. To conduct negotiations and evaluate collections, most archivists rely on field trips. These trips may be short visits to meet with one potential donor or an extended visit to see many prospects in a given locale. Whatever the scope of the particular trip, work in the field requires good organization and much advance planning: letters must be written, appointments scheduled, and background research done for on-site appraisals. The archivist must be prepared for a long workday. Because of donors' schedules, many appointments must be made after normal working hours. Once in the field, the archivist must be prepared for the frustration that comes with last-minute cancellations, waiting for return calls that never come, or discovering that the collection is fragmentary or of little value to the repository. The initial in-person contact with the donor is often a critical negotiating point, turning on how the agent and the repository's case are presented. The field archivist, armed with available information about the collection, its creator, and/or custodian, will also use the on-site visit to conduct an initial appraisal of the records' value.

Follow-Up Work to the Field Trip. Work in the field must be backed up with detailed paperwork in the office, not only in trip preparation but especially in handling the follow-up work generated by the trip. One important follow-up activity is preparing a detailed record of the completed trip, noting who was contacted, who could not be reached, and

Figure 5-3   Field Report

| **Northern Wisconsin** | **9/22/91** | **Mary Pickering** |

I arrived at Johnston's Lodge and Outfitters. Mark Johnston immediately gave me a tour. The resort was started by Mark's grandfather, William Johnston, who bought the land in 1910, shortly after it had been logged. He built the lodge in 1913, and built most of the cabins over the next thirty years. Charles Johnston, Mark's father, added a few cabins, but was best known for starting the outfitting side of the business. Mark took over in 1950.

After the tour, Johnston took me to the lodge attic where the records are stored. The collection falls into two major categories: business records and family records, although there is often no clear separation. The family correspondence, in particular, often deals with business affairs.

Business Records

The business records include guest registers dating to 1913 (3.5 cf). Register entries include the address of the patron, number of people in the party, reason for staying at the resort, and comments. The registers provide excellent documentation of resort patrons. The collection includes photographs (5 cf) of construction, equipment, resort activities, hunting and fishing trips, and the daily life both of the resort and its owners.

A second set of records dates to 1940 and includes financial information, publicity materials, equipment inventories, and trip planning files (4 cf). Although not complete, these records provide excellent documentation of fifty years of operations. The financial records also include receipts, purchase orders, vouchers and canceled checks dating to 1925 (15 cf).

I expressed our interest in all of the files except the routine financial materials which I suggested be destroyed. I explained that we are interested in the summary financial information because it is concise and complete. He seemed to accept this explanation, but we will probably need to repeat it.

Family Records

This is a letter writing family. The attic contains a consistent run of correspondence from 1890, when William Johnston arrived in New York from England, to 1953, when Mark returned from the Korean War and took over operation of the resort. The earliest letters are from Joseph Johnston, William's brother, describing Wisconsin's farm country and encouraging William to immigrate. The bulk of the correspondence is between family members when away from the resort describing family affairs and the resort business.

Donation

Johnston donated the resort registers, but wanted to review the correspondence for personal information before donating any other records. I explained our willingness to place a restriction on portions of the collection for some specific period of time, but he still wanted to consider the donation carefully. He will donate, but I am concerned that the collection may be "sanitized."

Report continues with details of other contacts made during trip.

---

what potential new leads were provided by existing contacts. The report also should contain a summary of discussions with each contact, including what commitments were made, what actions have to be taken as the result of the meeting, and what additional information or other assistance the field archivist has agreed to provide to the donor. (See Figure 5-3.) This record, traditionally in the form of a field report, is useful in keeping staff colleagues abreast of acquisition work, but its primary purpose is to provide an accurate record of the details of collecting activity. The field trip information, whether in note or report form, becomes part of the tracking process when it is entered in the individual lead record. In tidying up from the trip, the archivist must not forget those follow-up letters to potential donors that attest to the archivist's interest in their records and pleasure in meeting with them to discuss possible acquisition.

Donor Negotiations

If the archivist has determined that the records under consideration are of significant value and relate to other repository holdings, and if the donor is pleased with the prospective home for the material, the next step is negotiation for the records' physical and legal transfer. Sometimes this process may involve little more than executing a deed of gift and packing the papers for transfer. Just as likely, however, negotiations will be lengthy, and at times they will stall or be plagued by indecision. No matter how slowly negotiations proceed, the field representative must try to keep them on track. This phase of acquisition work calls for patience, diplomacy, and tact. It is critical that archivists establish their competence and credibility. They must have the donor's trust, whether dealing with sensitive and intimate personal and family papers or organizational records.

I'm giving my papers to the Junkmen's Institute of America.

Fred G. Sanford

To strengthen trust and confidence in the prospective repository, the archivist may refer the potential donor to established repository benefactors for an endorsement. Some collecting agencies routinely invite major prospects to visit the archives, to inspect the facilities, and to see how the staff cares for collections and how they are used. In dealing with donors with larger and more complex collections, particularly those of corporate organizations, the archivist should submit a formal acquisition proposal, even if it is not requested. This proposal should provide a rationale for repository placement, list the resources the depository will expend in organizing and preserving the collection, set a time-frame for processing the records, suggest provisions for access and restrictions, and spell out the amount of reference services the repository will extend to the donor. The proposal may also recommend acquisition options such as microfilming or deposit. Many of these matters will be dealt with in the deed of gift, and if negotiations are well along, a draft deed should be attached to the proposal. (For details on drafting a deed of gift, see Chapter 9.)

In negotiating, the field archivist must be prepared to discuss possible restrictions on collection access. Access restrictions are often critical to preserving the integrity of the collection. They can help prevent the donor from weeding files or transferring incomplete collections. They can give assurance to the donor that the personal privacy of living persons affected by the collection will be protected.[4]

---

[4] Access restrictions are discussed in Chapter 9.

An archivist explains to prospective donor Colonel Walter Choinski, career soldier and post-World War II military intelligence adviser, the advantages of and procedures for transferring his papers to the archives. (*Robert Granflaten, Courtesy of The State Historical Society of Wisconsin*)

The archivist is certain to be asked by many donors about provisions of the Internal Revenue Code affecting gifts of records. The solicitor needs to be conversant about the ever-changing tax law affecting such gifts. At present the tax law prohibits donors of self-created papers from claiming the "fair market value" of the collection as a tax deduction. For example, the novelist John Updike, who donated his papers to Harvard University, his alma mater, can only claim the costs incurred in creating the physical documents—the paper, ink and other supplies—and then only if they were not previously deducted as business expenses. If Updike's papers had been left to his estate or sold to another party, then the more fortunate new owners could claim a deduction. If a donor is to take a market-value tax deduction over $5,000, the papers must have an independent appraisal. Donors may contact the Society of American Archivists for its list of appraisers.[5] In informing the donors about provisions of the tax code, the archivist should urge them to consult with their attorney.

In the negotiations, the archivist should not overlook the donor as a source of financial support for subsequent processing and care of their collection. Preservation is expensive, and many potential donors are able and willing to provide a tax-deductible gift to cover some or all of these costs. Increasingly, archivists are requesting, if not requiring, that

---

[5] This list is published in *Society of American Archivists 1993 Directory of Consultants* (Chicago: Society of American Archivists, 1993).

corporate organizations underwrite the costs of processing and administering their donated records.[6]

Finally, what should the negotiator tell potential donors when their collections have proven financial value on the open market? Here archivists face
an ethical dilemma. The repository wants the collection as a gift, but are they not ethically bound to
inform donors when their papers have financial
worth? Or do archivists sidestep this ethical consideration by following one collector's observation: "If
they're not aware [of their papers' value], they can't
be very bright."[7] Archivists are to eschew this last
advice. Similarly, collections may include peripheral
material of considerable monetary value such as nu-
mismatic and philatelic material of which the donor
is unaware. The responsible field agent will notify
donors of such items and request their advice for
disposition.

Acquisition by Purchase

While collecting repositories build their holdings primarily through donations, some collections
are only available through purchase. Archivists
must, therefore, know how to deal with those record
creators or "custodians" with documents for sale.
Many repositories limit purchase, using it only as
an adjunct to collection-building. Purchasing some
letters of a literary figure, the corpus of whose work
the repository already holds, is one sensible example
of this situation. Some donors, their economic self-
interest heightened by the repository's interest, may
offer to sell their collection. Most acquisition by purchase, however, is done through rare book and manuscript dealers, either as agents for the seller or as
owners of the materials, and, to a lesser extent,
through major auction houses.

Dealers are, in effect, another source of leads
that can modestly assist the repository in collection
development. Field collectors should, therefore, receive dealers' catalogs that list material in their repository's area of interest. More importantly, they
should develop a professional relationship with dealers who may offer them first option to purchase or
put them in contact with potential donors whose
records have historical but not financial value or

Before donating his papers, news commentator Garrick Utley visits
the repository to see how the staff has administered the papers of
his father, radio and television commentator, Clifton Utley. (*Robert
Granflaten, Courtesy of State Historical Society of Wisconsin*)

who prefer donation to sale. Most dealers will send
small items on approval; large collections, of course,
must be evaluated by the field archivist *in situ*. The
dealer's asking price is often negotiable, especially
if the repository is the primary—if not the sole—
market for the materials.[8] Before making a major
expenditure—likely one involving several thousand
dollars in an already inflated market—the repository should get an independent appraisal of the collection's monetary value, particularly if its archivists are unfamiliar with the market. For major
purchases, some archival administrators turn to
benefactors who find the institution's acquisition of
a prestigious collection an alluring proposition.

Selling the Program: Collecting
Development Information Materials

Successful solicitation requires not only that
archivists know much about prospective donors, but
that the donors learn about the repository. To explain the archives' program and practices to potential donors, major collecting agencies prepare a brochure briefly describing collecting goals, specific
acquisition areas, and important repository holdings. Most brochures also describe collection care
and use, and specify whom to contact at the repository for further information or assistance. The best
of these promotional pieces are graphically illustrated and carry a succinct message.

---

[6] For basic issues archivists need to consider when negotiat-
ing for corporate records, see David J. Klaassen, "The Archival
Intersection: Cooperation between Collecting Repositories and
Nonprofit Organizations"; and Dennis E. Meissner, "Corporate
Records in Noncorporate Archives: A Case Study," *Midwestern
Archivist* 15 (1990), 25–38 and 39–50.

[7] Howard Gotlieb quoted in David Greenberg, "Floppy
Flop," *The New Republic*, 17 June 1991, 20.

[8] For further information on working with dealers, see
Mary Lynn McCree, "Good Sense and Good Judgment: Defining
Collections and Collecting," *Drexel Library Quarterly* 11 (January
1975), 28–32.

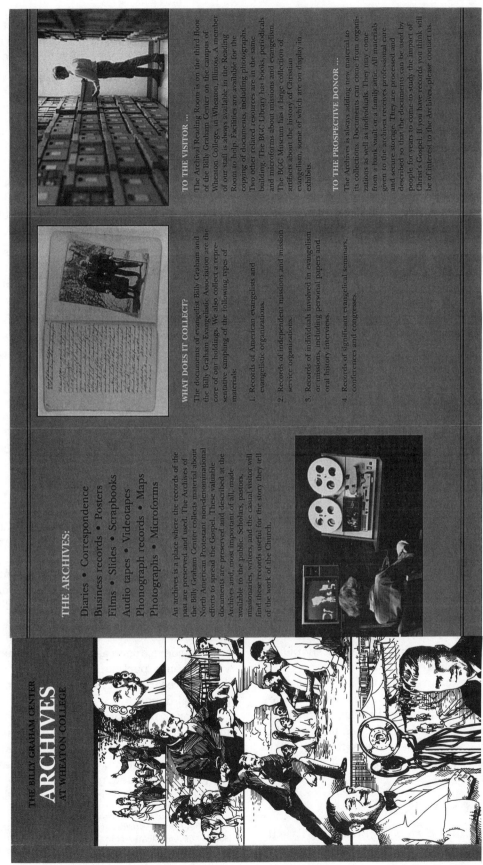

THE ARCHIVES:

Diaries • Correspondence
Business records • Posters
Films • Slides • Scrapbooks
Audio tapes • Videotapes
Phonograph records • Maps
Photographs • Microforms

An archive is a place where the records of the past are preserved and used. The Archives of the Billy Graham Center collects material about North American Protestant non-denominational efforts to spread the Gospel. These valuable documents are preserved and described at the Archives and, most important of all, made available to the public. Scholars, pastors, missionaries, writers, and the casual visitor will find these records useful for the story they tell of the work of the Church.

WHAT DOES IT COLLECT?

The documents of evangelist Billy Graham and the Billy Graham Evangelistic Association are the core of our holdings. We also collect a representative sampling of the following types of materials:

1. Records of American evangelists and evangelistic organizations.

2. Records of independent missions and mission service organizations.

3. Records of individuals involved in evangelism or missions, including personal papers and oral history interviews.

4. Records of significant evangelical seminars, conferences and congresses.

TO THE VISITOR ...

The Archival Reading Room is on the third floor of the Billy Graham Center on the campus of Wheaton College, in Wheaton, Illinois. A member of our staff is always available in the Reading Room to help. Facilities are available for the copying of documents, including photographs. Two other related resources are in the same building. The BGC Library has books, periodicals and microforms about missions and evangelism. The BGC Museum has a large collection of artifacts about the history of Christian evangelism, some of which are on display in its exhibits.

TO THE PROSPECTIVE DONOR ...

The Archives is always adding new material to its collections. Documents can come from organizations as well as individuals. They may come from a bank vault or a family attic. All materials given to the archives receives professional care and secure storage. They are processed and described so that the documents can be used by people for years to come to study the impact of Christ's Gospel. If you have records you think will be of interest to the Archives, please contact us.

THE BILLY GRAHAM CENTER
ARCHIVES
AT WHEATON COLLEGE

A brochure from the Billy Graham Center Archives at Wheaton College, Wheaton, Illinois.

The brochure is designed to elicit general interest in the repository collecting program. Many donors will want more detailed information about the repository or its parent institution. Many repositories have a range of informational material that expands on the goals and programs of the institution. Some archivists provide potential donors with copies of their repository's collection guides or inventories to establish the repository's credentials and to further interest the potential donor.

Cultivating Established Donors

Good donor relations are an essential factor in a successful solicitation program. Following an initial donation, the archives can expect many future accessions from professionally active persons or from operating organizations for whom the archives is a designated repository. The donor relationship should not be transitory. This group is potentially one of the program's greatest assets. To capitalize on these assets, the repository needs to cultivate donors so they develop an abiding interest in the repository program. Donors should be recognized. A letter of appreciation, preferably from the head of the institution, should be sent following the receipt of each accession. (See Figure 5-4.) Some repositories recognize donors by an annual listing of their names in an institutional publication. Some send a formal certificate acknowledging the gift. One institution, at Christmastime, sends its major donors a copy of its yearly calendar illustrated with photographs from the collections. Some repositories will recognize the donors of an exceptional acquisition with a formal opening of the papers or an exhibit drawn from the acquisition. All donors should receive a copy of the finding aid to their collection.

Donors should be informed about institutional activities and invited to special events. If there is a newsletter, annual report, quarterly journal, or some other publication, donors' names should be added to the appropriate mailing list.

Not only are donors often the single most important source of entree to other collections, they also are an important source of financial support. In addition to requesting funding for the processing of their materials, many repositories regularly inform donors of the archives' special financial needs with gratifying results.

The Ethics of Solicitation

More than any other area of archival activity, the pursuit of coveted collections has led to charges and countercharges of ethical misconduct of archivists and their institutions. Most archivists now subscribe to the following as an ethical guide to acquisition:

- Archivists should not compete when competition would endanger the safety or violate the integrity of a collection.

- Archivists should not accept accessions for which they lack the resources to properly administer and make available to the public.

- Archivists, when offered material that is out of scope of the repository's stated field of interest, should suggest a more appropriate repository for the donor's consideration.

- When two or more institutions are soliciting the same donor, their representatives should not unjustly disparage the facilities or intentions of others.

- Finally, archivists should not make commitments they cannot fulfill and should faithfully observe all agreements made at the time of acquisition.[9]

Summary

The records kept by individuals and families and by most organizations are not subject to the pre-archival control provided by a records management program. To identify, evaluate, and bring these records into repository custody, archivists employ a method called field collecting.

With the acquisitions policy as a framework, archivists need to examine various sources of leads to potential collections and their donors and then develop short-term plans to pursue these leads.

To track potential collections, archivists use an information system consisting of a lead record of prospective donors, a case file containing the documentation generated as the lead is pursued, and a tracking device such as a tickler file that alerts archivists when a particular action should be taken. A detailed record must be kept of all contacts with the potential donor.

Donor negotiation is the most important step in the solicitation process. The archival negotiator needs diplomatic skill, a strategic grasp of the complex issues involved, restraint in making commitments, and, frequently, the assistance of legal counsel. The field collector also needs to know when to

[9] *A Code of Ethics for Archivists and Commentary* (Chicago: Society of American Archivists, 1992); and Philip P. Mason, "The Ethics of Collecting," *Georgia Archive,* (Winter 1977), 36–50.

Figure 5-4 Repository Letter Acknowledging Donation of Records

THE STATE HISTORICAL SOCIETY OF WISCONSIN

H. Nicholas Muller III, Director

816 State Street
Madison, Wisconsin 53706-1488
608/264-6400
FAX: 608/264-6404

October 15, 1991

Mr. Mark Johnston
1345 Washburn Road
Cable, WI 54701

Dear Mr. Johnston:

Mary Pickering just informed me of your recent donation of guest registers from Johnston's Lodge. I want to express my appreciation for this generous contribution to the collections of the State Historical Society of Wisconsin. It is only through the interest shown by people such as yourself that we are able to document the state's heritage.

Ms. Pickering also mentioned that you have preserved an excellent collection of other records documenting your family and the operation of your resort. I hope that you will give serious thought to donating additional resort records, photographs, and family letters. If future generations are to understand Wisconsin history, they must understand family life, settlement, and tourism in northern Wisconsin. The records kept by your family will be critical to the development of any adequate history of Cable and the surrounding region.

Once again, I want to thank you for donating the guest registers. I hope that this donation will be the beginning of a growing collection of Johnston family materials at the State Historical Society.

Sincerely,

H. Nicholas Muller III

call on others to provide donor entree and assist with negotiations.

The donor is the repository's best friend, providing leads and entree to potential donors, often supporting the acquisition program with financial assistance, and in other ways supporting the archives' mission. Ensuring the on-going support of these donors is a high priority.

Selected Readings

Kenneth W. Duckett, *Modern Manuscripts* (Nashville: American Association for State and Local History, 1975), 3–20, 56–85.

John A. Fleckner, *Archives & Manuscripts: Surveys* (Chicago: Society of American Archivists, 1977).

David J. Klaassen. "The Archival Intersection: Cooperation between Collecting Repositories and Nonprofit Organizations," *Midwestern Archivist* 15 (1990), 25–38.

Philip P. Mason, "The Ethics of Collecting," *Georgia Archive* 5 (Winter 1977), 36–50.

Mary Lynn McCree, "Good Sense and Good Judgement: Defining Collections and Collecting," *Drexel Library Quarterly* 11 (January 1975), 28–32.

Dennis E. Meissner, "Corporate Records in Noncorporate Archives: A Case Study," *Midwestern Archivist* 15 (1990), 39–50.

Virgina R. Stewart, "A Primer on Manuscript Field Work," *The Midwestern Archivist* 1 (1976); 3–20. This article remains a classic on archival field collecting.

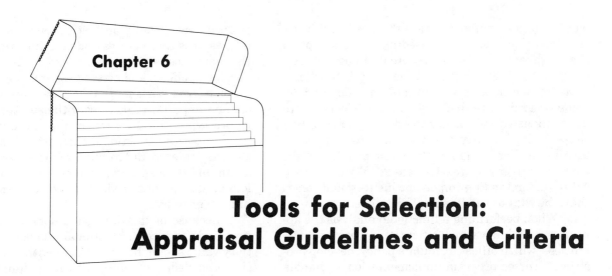

Chapter 6

Tools for Selection:
Appraisal Guidelines and Criteria

An acquisitions policy defines what archivists should acquire in terms of information—what activities and subjects they should document. Appraisal is a process by which archivists evaluate how well specific records contribute to policy objectives. The two, acquisitions policy and records appraisal, must be integrated to ensure that a particular accession is compatible with institutional documentation goals.

The Five Analyses of Archival Appraisal

There are five analyses that make up the basic tools archivists need in their appraisal kits to identify and select records of enduring value. These are an analysis

- of a record's functional characteristics—who made the record and for what purpose;

- of the information in the record to determine its significance and quality;

- of the record in the context of parallel or related documentary sources;

- of the potential uses that are likely to be made of the record and the physical, legal, and intellectual limitations on access;

- of the cost of preserving the record weighed against the benefit of retaining the information.[1]

This chapter examines these five analyses in detail and discusses their application. It also consid-

ers the intrinsic value of a record as an appraisal criteria and discusses special requirements for appraising visual, sound, and machine-readable records.

Functional Analysis: Evaluating the Importance of the Record's Original Purpose. The use of functional analysis, that is, an examination of who created the record and for what purpose, is based on the premise that archivists must understand the relationship between the records and the institution's functions if they are to understand the record's significance. Many archivists believe that functional analysis is the best way to document institutions.[2]

In conducting this analysis, the archivist needs to ask three basic questions:

- At what level of policy-making and executive direction in the administrative hierarchy is the office or person that created the records?

- What are the significant functions of the organizational unit or person that created the records?

- What records are most closely related to and best document significant functions?

In answering these questions, the archivist examines factors that are largely external to the content of the record itself.

Significance of the records creator's position in the organizational hierarchy. This first component of functional analysis helps the archivist determine

---

[1] These five analyses basically follow the taxonomy in Boles, *Archival Appraisal*, 20–21.

[2] This analysis also provides some of the tools necessary to carry out the "institutional functional analysis" described in Chapter 3.

what offices or persons create the most archivally significant records. It is based on the assumption that high-level offices usually create important records because they carry out the most basic functions; that decision makers who formulate policy and develop programs are likely to create or receive more comprehensive and substantive documentation than those levels of activity which oversee program implementation. For example, the main administrative files of a university president are usually more critical to understanding important institutional issues than the files of the financial aid office.

When performing a functional analysis the appraiser must know which offices have what responsibilities—which offices formulate policy, develop programs, oversee program implementation, or handle the administrative housekeeping chores. The administrative placement of these activities varies from institution to institution, depending upon their historical development and the degree of administrative centralization. The archivist, therefore, must understand the unique organizational structure of a particular institution. Important offices nonetheless create many records that are unimportant. Thus, while organizational structure can offer clues to the value of records, by itself it can also be misleading. Therefore, the appraiser needs to know more than the position of the office creating the records.

Significance of the records creator's functions. This analysis helps the archivist determine the relationship between a particular unit's function and the institutional functions and activities that the acquisition policy determines should be documented. This analysis is usually premised on the assumption that the most important functions and activities of an organization will generate the most important organizational records. Therefore, the archivist needs to know the overall mission of the organization and what functions are carried out by each office or other organizational unit in an institution. By examining the unit's functions and activities and comparing them to those identified as critical in the acquisitions policy, the archivist develops clues as to the significance of the unit's records.

Significance of the records. This third element of functional analysis assists the archivist in determining what records best document the archives' acquisition goals. Here a knowledge of the record's function—what it was created to document—helps measure its significance. Determining the original purpose of a record is not, however, enough. The function of the record must be closely related to the institutional duties and activities the archives seeks

to document, usually an institution's core responsibilities. It is these duties and activities that provide the most substantive evidence of how an institution develops policies and strategies, and carries out its mission. Archivists must take care, however, not to confuse important functions with usually significant record types. Minutes, for example, are among the most important functional categories of records archivists preserve. But minutes of meetings regarding an unimportant activity, such as renovating the staff lounge, document a trivial function and are thus not important to retain.

Because of the linkages among creator, function, and the record, functional analysis for evidentiary value should be undertaken with a comprehensive knowledge of an institution's functions and programs and the documentation they produce. If possible, functional analysis should not be undertaken through a piecemeal or bottom-up examination of a specific activity or set of records. Properly applied, functional analysis is the bulwark of institutional records appraisal.

Functional analysis can also be applied to the papers and records of individuals. It provides a framework for examining the various positions a person held throughout a career, the significant functions associated with those positions, and the papers that are most closely connected with and best document the activities and duties in carrying out a particular function. For personal papers, the premise is the same: important people have important duties and responsibilities that in turn generate important papers. In collecting repositories, however, appraisers too seldom apply functional analysis to personal papers or to records of organizations cut loose from their institutional moorings.

One of the great assets of functional analysis is that it is a cost-effective approach to determine the evidential value of the record. Rather than examining the informational content of massive record series, the archivist need only analyze the external evidentiary characteristics of the record series as a whole.

The process has limitations. The emphasis of functional analysis on hierarchical structure may obscure the value of some records needed for institutional accountability or history. The flow of information within bureaucratic organizations does not always follow the vertical lines of hierarchical organization, and hence, does not always fit Schellenberg's "tip of the iceberg" appraisal model where records documenting policy formulation and executive direction are assumed to exist largely at the top of the organizational pyramid. An examination of an organization's communication system is the primary mechanism through which the mix of vertical and horizontal information flow can be determined.[3] Further, what makes functional analysis cost-effective is also a major weakness of the process. Archivists often rely too much on an analysis of functional characteristics to determine a record's value rather than on an examination of the record content. Functional analysis only works when evidentiary and informational values overlap. Though used as such, it is not a substitute for content analysis.[4]

Content Analysis: Evaluating a Record's Informational Significance. While functional analysis provides important clues to the value of a record, especially for institutional history, it is less useful in evaluating what Schellenberg called "informational" value—what records tell us about people, places, and phenomena with which the institution dealt. A functional analysis of personnel files of railroad workers on the Northern Pacific Railway, 1909 to the 1960s, would probably conclude that the records were housekeeping documents tracking an employee's tenure and status with the company and of marginal evidential value. An analysis of their content, on the other hand, discloses a wealth of demographic, economic, and social information about a particular population.[5] For many archival programs, the records of greatest importance are those that contain information on social, economic, and political concerns. Most researchers are more interested in the objects of bureaucratic activity rather than the activity itself. For example, many researchers request the Wisconsin Department of Civil Preparedness files on natural disasters but few, if any, call for the agency's administrative records.

In analyzing informational content, the archivist needs to answer two basic questions:

- How significant are the subjects or topics documented in the records as defined through the repository acquisition policy?

- How well do the records document those subjects?

Significance of the subject. Determining significance is among the most elusive objectives of archi-

Archivists analyze photos for subject significance. (*Sisters of Providence Archives, Seattle, Washington*)

val appraisal. To use Schellenberg's words, it is "in the realm of the imponderable." One criteria that can be used to define significance is how well the information in the record meets acquisition goals defined in the institutional collecting policy. "The more closely the basic topics of a particular set of records coincide with . . . core collecting goals," Boles observes, "the more valuable the material is to . . . [the] archives."[6] Even fragmentary documentation on key areas is more important than voluminous documentation on out-of-scope concerns. In evaluating the informational significance of the Northern Pacific Railroad personnel files, the archivist would note that the records document the railroad worker, that the documentation contains information on nationality, age, and nativity, as well as a detailed employment history including wages. If documenting a laboring group at a micro-level is within the institutional acquisition policy, then these records would likely meet the criteria for significance.

The quality of the documentation. In evaluating how well the records document those subjects de-

[3] See JoAnne Yates, "Internal Communication Systems in American Business Structures: A Framework to Aid Appraisal," *American Archivist* 48 (Spring 1985), 141–58.

[4] Boles, *Archival Appraisal*, 100.

[5] Accession Record, No. Mss. 7-23-81 (1981), Personnel Files, Northern Pacific Railway Company Records, Minnesota Historical Society.

[6] Boles, *Archival Appraisal*, 34.

fined as of interest by institutional policy, the archivist needs to consider (1) the completeness of the record, (2) the time span it covers, and (3) the general quality of information. The archivist determines the quality of the information by asking how detailed or concentrated is the data on a subject, what is the range of relevant subjects covered, and how significant and closely related is the creator of the records to the subjects they document?

Timespan and completeness are significant because records that are complete and cover a long time period allow researchers to discover trends and draw more valid conclusions. Especially useful are records with extended and unbroken time series data offering uniform and thus comparable information. Archivists should note when records have missing segments or chronological gaps and consider if and how these limitations impair the information's usefulness. How do the Northern Pacific Railway's personnel files meet the criteria of completeness and timespan? The 210,100 files cover approximately eighty percent of the employees of the Northern Pacific Railway from 1909 to the 1960s, with some work history information dating back to the 1880s. The files are fairly complete and uniform but would be of even greater importance if none of the early files were missing.

Approximate completeness is not enough; completeness also should relate to the time period when the subject was most significant. The personnel files document the railroad worker during the maturation of western railroad enterprise and during an important period of Eastern European immigration to the northwestern states. Unfortunately, however, the records of many phenomena such as social and political movements frequently are most fragmentary when the movement is most active.

Context Analysis: Examining the Significance of the Record in Relation to Other Documentary Sources. Today's documentary environment is replete with redundant information. Therefore, it is necessary to appraise records in comparison with other available information sources. In this third analysis the archivist asks the following:

- How unique is the physical record; is it duplicated in the creating agency or elsewhere?

- If the record exists in several forms, is there a preferred form for retention?

- How unique is the information in the record and how does it compare in scope and quality with information found in related sources?

- Is the record an acceptable substitute for a preferred record that is not available for retention?

- Can the information in the record be linked with other records in ways that will enhance its usefulness?

- How scarce is the documentation on a subject?

Several criteria guide this comparative analysis:

Record duplication. The physical duplication of records is a characteristic of our information age. This duplication is found everywhere in modern bureaucracy. Field office files are often replicated in home office files. Records documenting local functions such as school censuses or municipal audits are also filed with state governments, and copies of many state records are filed with the federal government. Many private organizations such as labor unions and fraternal or service organizations—the American Red Cross is an example—operate on a national, regional, state, and local level. At each level, the files often contain reports, minutes, and other documents from the other organizational levels. The archivist needs to know where the original record is created and if it is being preserved. Where multiple copies of records exist within a bureaucratic organization, the archivist will usually accession the copy from the originating office.

Preferred format of the record. Records often exist in more than one format. Today's technology has greatly simplified the transfer of information from one medium to another and, as a result, the same information often exists in several formats. The Wisconsin statewide public school census, for example, is available in a machine-readable data file, a computer-generated paper copy, and as computer output microfiche (COM). Based on factors such as cost of preservation, maintenance, and type of use and ease of access, the archivist must determine in which format or formats records should be retained.

Uniqueness of the information. Even though a physical record is unique, the information it contains is often found elsewhere. Information is duplicated by parallel documentation. For example, if an archivist accessioned the local daily television news produced by three stations in his city, the result would be three unique record series with similar information about the same events. Though each news program is unique, most of the information is redundant.

Information is also duplicated through aggregation and summarization. A great deal of statistical and financial data is reported weekly, monthly, quarterly, and annually. Often wards, townships, cities, counties, or planning districts summarize the same information at several levels of aggregation. Special studies of bureaucratic task forces based on questionnaire, interview, and investigative data are issued in a final composite report which is often published. In many cases, aggregation and summarization render the raw data of little value, but in other cases it can be used for additional analysis. Further, for the researcher seeking highly specific or itemized data, summaries are of no value. No genealogist will accept federal census summaries in lieu of the original marshal's returns. Seasoned appraisers use knowledge of research use and preservation costs to judge when summarized or disaggregated information is needed.[7]

Given the increasing ease of publishing in print or near-print formats, much information that was heretofore the domain of the archivist now appears in print. It is essential, therefore, that archivists be knowledgeable about associated printed materials within their field of acquisition and the extent to which they duplicate information in archival records.

Determining the degree of information overlap and redundancy and the best source of information is difficult, for it requires a comprehensive knowledge of the appraiser's own repository's holdings and the broader published and unpublished "universe of documentation." The "universe of documentation" is an abstraction, and, while archivists must be knowledgeable about parallel and related documentation in their area of acquisitions, attempting to compare one accession with the totality of information on the subject is a fool's errand.

Record substitution. Before appraisers reject records on the grounds that fuller or more pertinent information exists, they must first determine if the preferred records are available or feasible for retention. If they are not, the records under appraisal may be a substitute. For example, some governmental archives save important records series documenting business. Government records regarding taxation and wealth, incorporation, licensing and regulation, and labor and consumer protection partially substitute for business documentation unavailable from the private sector.

Record linkage. This term, as commonly used in social science research, refers to the ability to combine data on identical or similar cases (often an individual) from two or more sources using common identifiers such as name, age, sex, place of residence, or social security number. The concept of linkage is particularly important in appraising social and economic data. For example, when census records are linked with vital statistics, naturalization records, and school records, they can (as any genealogist knows) reveal a great deal about ethnicity, mobility, marriage, fertility, family size and structure, and mortality. Linking this information with court cases on divorce reveals much about family disintegration. Linkage enhanced the appraisers' estimate of the value of the Northern Pacific Railway personnel files when they determined the records could be linked with census, compiled military service, and pension records in the National Archives. Appraising records for their linkage value is difficult, but linkage is an important reason for sometimes preserving routine records such as property tax rolls.

A second type of record linkage is what Boles calls "the web of interrelated information" created by a well-focused acquisitions program. Here the archivist is interested in how the information in a particular accession relates to previously accessioned information. The papers of one Italian immigrant, to use Boles' example, may be of interest, but a broader collection of immigrant materials on Italians, including personal accounts, ethnic school and church records, fraternal organization records, and ethnic newspaper files "assume a collective importance . . . greater than the individual parts."[8] The New York State Archives and Records Administration incorporated the same viewpoint by acknowledging that there is an "increased possibility" that records series which complement holdings already in the State Archives will be accessioned.[9]

Scarcity of the records. The scarcity of documentation is another criteria for evaluating records. An archival dictum is that "old age in records is to be respected." It is scarcity, however, that is to be revered. Because of the scarcity of older materials, many archives have adopted arbitrary time periods—1865 is a common one—before which all records are retained. But age and scarcity are not always linked. In 1964, the State Historical Society of Wisconsin disposed of large quantities of essentially

[7] For criteria used to evaluate statistical records, see Meyer H. Fishbein, "Reflections on Appraising Statistical Records," *American Archivist* 50 (Spring 1987), 226–34.

[8] Boles, *Archival Appraisal*, 41.

[9] Draft of New York State Archives Appraisal Manual, May 6, 1986, 10.

As a result of a fire that raged through the New York State Capitol, destroying the State Library, pre-1911 public records are scarce. (*Courtesy of the New York State Archives and Records Administration*)

duplicate Civil War records. The records were old but they were not scarce. In contrast, New York State suffered the loss of major archival assets when the state capitol burned in 1911. As a consequence, state records predating the fire, even if not comparatively old, are scarce. Rarity is as much a factor of natural disasters and past records dispositions as it is of age. Like the archaeologist who salvages fragmentary bones from an ancient past, the archivist is more likely to save random bits and pieces of records from the period or for a topic where there is a paucity of other documentation. Scarcity enhances the value of even the most routine documents.

To repeat the questions listed at the beginning of this section, the appraiser in doing a context analysis needs to ask: (1) is the record physically duplicated elsewhere? (2) if the record is in several formats, which is best for the long-term retention and use of the information? (3) is the information in the record duplicated by parallel documentation elsewhere, by the process of aggregation and summarization, or by published sources? (4) is the record an acceptable substitute for the preferred source of the information which is unavailable? (5) do the records complement or can they be linked to other information sources in the repository and elsewhere? and (6) how scarce are the records?

Analysis of Accessibility and Use. The archivist needs to consider the usefulness of the records in meeting the needs of his repository's clientele as well as any physical, intellectual, and legal impediments to access that would diminish their usefulness. Evaluating record value based on past, present, and, especially, future use is elusive and difficult. The concept troubles archivists who believe that use is too immediate and short-term a consideration to employ in selecting for posterity. Yet, it is difficult to justify committing scarce resources for the retention of records without some prospect of their being used. Without use, archives have no value.

In evaluating the usefulness of a record, the archivist needs to ask the following:

• How does the record meet the information needs and interests of various user groups served by the repository?

• What is the potential utility of the record based on past and present research use?

• What are the physical, intellectual, or legal barriers in making the record accessible?

The repository's clientele. The research interests of the repository's users are intimately linked to the institution's acquisition policy. If a business corporation sets up an archives primarily for the use of management, then it is very likely that the major use will be of those legal and administrative records important to the continuity and protection of corporate life. In this appraisal environment, the older closed files of terminated employees, such as those of the Northern Pacific Railway, would have no future value. The other end of the spectrum is the large-scale public use of archival sources by genealogists, community historians, and avocational users generally. For these users, the archivist is more likely to accession files of highly itemized information about individuals—census data, probate and naturalization records, and, for some fortunate researchers, personnel files of their forebears.

Past and projected use. Archivists are also enjoined to consider the past, current, and potential use of archival records in appraising a collection for its research value. Maynard Brichford urges archivists to hold their independent judgment in abeyance and read their collection use statistics, which are "one of the best indicators of research value," providing as they do the "collective judgment" of the full-range of past users of archival records.[10] Many appraisers also recommend using research trends in scholarly disciplines as a guide in evaluating a record's research potential. Predicting future research use, other archivists believe, is the domain of the seer and mystic, not the appraiser.

Use analysis is most helpful to those institutional repositories with well-defined (and often limited) acquisition goals or to those collecting archives with a sharply focused area of research— whether immigration history, a presidential administration, or genealogy and local history. If appraisers are to rely on use statistics and patterns, they should also compare their data with that of repositories with similar acquisition fields, for use statistics can be misleading when they validate nothing more than that researchers use what records are available.

[10] Maynard J. Brichford, *Archives & Manuscripts: Appraisal & Accessioning* (Chicago: Society of American Archivists, 1977), 9.

Some archivists believe that use statistics are a good indicator of research value. (*Courtesy of the Massachusetts Archives*)

The accessibility of the records and/or information. The third criterion asks how accessible the records are to the researcher. The major impediments to accessibility are legal and administrative restrictions on use of the records and physical and intellectual barriers in the records themselves.

Severe and long-term restrictions on access greatly diminish the research value of records. Archivists find that legal and administrative restrictions on access have limited or prohibited the use of important documentation on such matters as poverty and wealth, crime and punishment, business and financial dealings, and political and diplomatic affairs. Some of these records will eventually be opened but others are restricted indefinitely. Even so, only the foolish appraiser will be guided solely by access limitations. Where legal and administrative restrictions are unreasonable, archivists need to work for revision. Through negotiation and revision of laws and regulations, it is often possible to provide limited access to such records or even remove the restrictions. The State Historical Society of Wisconsin, for example, has negotiated use agreements for historically rich but legally confidential sources such as corporate income tax returns, banking examiner reports, and corrections case files. In appraising such records, the archivist must weigh other appraisal criteria against the severity of the restriction and/ or the costs of removing legal and administrative barriers to access.

We should not bequeath puzzles to posterity.

Maynard J. Brichford, *Archives & Manuscripts: Appraisal & Accessioning*, 1977

There also are physical and intellectual barriers to access which the archivist must confront. These barriers are many: accessions with no defined structure or in a disorganized state; texts, sound recordings, or visual images that are illegible or unrecognizable; accounting work papers, scientific data, stenographic notes, and other records that will require painstaking effort to read or which may be undecipherable; and records that depend on obsolescent technology to make them intelligible. The sheer volume of an accession can both impede physical access and bury important kernels of information in tons of chaff. Where access is dependent upon related indexes, filing codes, or, in the case of electronic records, software and program documentation, the archivist and researcher must have access to these tools if the records are to be usable. Some of these barriers can be removed though extensive work, but the archivist must count the cost.

Cost-Benefit Analysis: Weighing the Value of the Information against the Cost of Preservation. Before the appraisal is complete, the archivist must weigh the value of the information against retention costs. Nearly fifty years ago archivists were told that "a stern and true cost accounting is a prerequisite of all orderly appraisal."[11] Few archivists, however, include the cost of record acquisition, processing, preservation, and retention into their evaluation. Rather, they treat these costs as undefined expenses and assume they are the cost of doing business. In an age of documentary overabundance, archivists must "attach a price tag" to their appraisal decisions.

In conducting a cost-benefit analysis the appraiser needs to ask the following:

- What are the costs of identifying, appraising, and accessioning the records?

- What are the costs of processing the acquisition to an affordable level?

- What are the costs for affordable preservation treatment?

Preservation costs are part of a cost-benefit analysis. (*Courtesy of the Massachusetts Archives*)

- What are the annual costs of housing the original records or reducing their bulk by microfilming or sampling?

Appraisal and accessioning costs. Often overlooked as an expense in the selection process, these costs can be very high when archivists contend with larger and more complex accessions. Some records systems are so voluminous or complex that the appraisal becomes a major expense. The National Archives 1981 appraisal of the Federal Bureau of Investigation files cost in excess of $500,000.[12] Where record surveys and inventories are needed to make the appraisal, their costs should be included in the cost-benefit analysis, as should all costs associated with donor negotiations and record accessioning, including packing and shipping costs. The estimated cost of appraisal and accessioning can be a factor in rejecting records before they are even evaluated.

For the archivist, appraisal costs are a conundrum. Without the resources to conduct a comprehensive evaluation of the records, the archivist cannot know their value. If archivists do not know the value of the records they cannot determine if an exhaustive appraisal is merited. Further, it is silly to evaluate costs before determining the information's value. Consequently, archivists try to limit appraisal costs, particularly of case files and other large volume records, by conducting a generic and often superficial review of the records that focuses on their functional characteristics rather than content. When the appraisal is inadequate, the repository either loses worthwhile records or incurs greater ex-

---

[11] G. Philip Bauer, *The Appraisal of Current and Recent Records* (National Archives Staff Information Circular No. 13, 1946).

[12] See pages 75–76.

Microfilm can provide cost savings, security, and wider use but the initial cost is an important appraisal consideration. The 32 cubic feet of records on the back wall (left) reduce to little more than a cubic foot of microfilm (right). (*Courtesy of Leonard Axelrod [left] and Robert Granflaten [right], State Historical Society of Wisconsin*)

penses in later phases of the collection's management by failing to discriminate in its selection.

Processing costs. Usually, processing costs are the largest short-term expense in preparing records for use. Processing costs include professional and paraprofessional staff time and also the cost of supplies. Processing costs are directly related to the organization of the records. If the records were generated in an institution with a program for files design and management, they may need very little reorganization, may arrive with file-level finding aids, and can be made quickly available for use. Unfortunately, the files of many organizations and individuals are chaotically arranged, intermingling important and trivial documentation. Under these circumstances, the value of the records must be great to justify the expense of processing. The New York State Archives appraisers, for example, are directed to reject "totally unorganized records series . . . unless there are compelling considerations demanding otherwise."[13]

Preservation costs. Most collection-level preservation is performed during processing. The repository staff, as part of the appraisal process, should determine the type of preservation needed and the personnel, supplies, and, in some cases, contract services required to stabilize the collection. At one extreme, these costs may involve item deacidification and encapsulation or even more expensive efforts to conserve documents with intrinsic value. More likely, given the mass of modern documents, the staff will recommend some form of information transfer

such as preservation microfilming a collection of paper records, in whole or part, or copying sound and visual records onto a more stable and usable medium. For selected portions of the collection, such as those segments with decaying papers or newsprint, many repositories use electrostatic copying on to archival-quality bond paper.

Cost of storing records or reducing their volume. Archivists cannot ignore the implications of their appraisal decisions on future storage needs and costs. While archivists can determine the current annual storage costs per cubic foot of materials, they cannot really calculate the costs of an open-ended acquisition. How would a state archivist, for example, measure the cost of storing indefinitely the legislature's bill-drafting records currently growing at an annual rate of twenty cubic feet? The archival manager, however, can calculate storage needs and costs for a fixed period of time—five, ten, twenty years, for example. This management exercise should shock archivists with the consequences of past and current commitments on future resources. The appraiser must also determine whether the acquisition will increase the need for special storage, including low-temperature vault space for color film or special areas for the storage of magnetic tapes and archival microfilm masters.

What archivists can determine more precisely is the most economical way to store records. For many records series, the appraiser needs to weigh alternatives to the permanent retention of records in their original form. One option is microfilming or some other form of information transfer. Microfilming costs are specific and provide the repository with

---

[13] Draft of New York State Archives Appraisal Manual, 14.

The symbolic value of some items makes them especially appropriate for exhibits. (*Association of American Medical Colleges*)

a baseline figure against which to evaluate storage options and costs. When the costs of microfilming are amortized over time, microfilming almost always becomes cost-effective. It offers preservation and reference access benefits as well. Cost estimates should include all expenses associated with the preparation and microfilming of the records.

Another option to reduce the bulk of an accession is to draw a sample or extensively weed the accession.[14] Though weeding and sampling are expensive and often complex, they can greatly reduce preservation and storage costs. The archivist needs to include the expense of designing and implementing sampling or weeding into the cost-benefit equation. These expenses may be assumed under the cost of processing.

Better pre-archival management of the records and more rigorous appraisal can significantly reduce subsequent collection management costs. The level of processing, degree of preservation treatment, and type of storage should depend upon the importance of the records to the repository, mandated retention, and anticipated use. Ultimately, however, archivists must accept the fact that some records, no matter how valuable and accessible, may be too expensive to retain.

Selecting Records for their Intrinsic Value

The intrinsic value of a record is seldom included in a list of appraisal criteria, but it should be. According to the *SAA Glossary,* intrinsic value is the value inherent in a document because of "some unique factor, such as age, content, usage, or circumstances surrounding its creation, signature, or attached seals" that requires the permanent retention of the document in its original physical form.

[14] See Chapter 8.

The qualities and characteristics defining intrinsic value also include the study of the physical form as evidence of technological development—a daguerreotype or letterpress copybook are examples. Intrinsic value may also come from aesthetic or artistic quality such as a Frank Lloyd Wright architectural sketch. It may come from the association of the record with famous people, places, and events such as the original manuscript of John F. Kennedy's 1961 inaugural address, or from high-level policy formulations with broad impact such as the United Nations Charter.[15] The documents of greatest intrinsic value, of course, are national symbols such as the Declaration of Independence and the Gettysburg Address.

Qualities and Characteristics of Records with Intrinsic Value

1. Physical form that may be subject for study if the records provide meaningful documentation or significant examples of the form.
2. Aesthetic or artistic quality.
3. Unique or curious physical features.
4. Age that provides a quality of uniqueness.
5. Value for use in exhibits.
6. Questionable authenticity, date, author, or other characteristic that is significant and ascertainable by physical examination.
7. General and substantial public interest because of direct association with famous or historically significant people, places, things, issues, or events.
8. Significance as documentation of the establishment or continuing legal basis of an agency or institution.
9. Significance as documentation of the formulation of policy at the highest executive levels when the policy has significance and broad effect throughout or beyond the agency or institution.

Intrinsic Value in Archival Material, 1982

Appraising Special Classes of Records

Most discussions about archival appraisal have focused on written records. Archivists today, however, have to appraise an expanding variety of information formats. Among these formats are (1) electronic or machine-readable records, (2) still photographs, (3) moving images, (4) sound records,

[15] *Intrinsic Value of Archival Material.* Staff Information Paper, No. 21 (Washington, D.C.: National Archives and Records Service, 1982), 1–6.

Technical Issues. In appraising the many forms of moving and still images, sound recordings, and electronic records, there are a series of technical issues the archivist needs to consider. These issues include the physical stability and long-term viability of current records; the ability to transfer the information from a decaying or obsolete medium to a newer one; and the effect of technological obsolescence on the future usability of the material. The archivist needs to know the following:

• Is the medium stable in its current form? That is, will it remain essentially unchanged or degrade at a predictable rate in an archival environment over a long period of time (100 years or more) without additional preservation treatment? What is the quality or condition of the medium as it stands? In a photograph, for instance, is the paper base so brittle that the image is endangered? In a photographic negative, is the silver that makes the image decaying or are stains in the clear area so strong that ordinary black and white printing techniques cannot be used? Are the color dyes in a motion picture fading? Has a data storage or video tape become so worn or otherwise degraded that the records are rendered unreadable? Even if the medium appears to be in good condition, does it have an inherent instability which would cause rapid degradation of the medium such as that found in nitrate and older acetate film or the emulsion binders in magnetic recording tape? Will the information be there at some point in the near future?

• When the information in the record needs to be transferred to a more stable medium for preservation and access, can this transfer be done satisfactorily? Even when it is technically possible to make an information transfer, will it be affordable or justifiable in view of other repository priorities? Most repositories do not have adequate resources for the continuous transfer of information from obsolete to new formats. The current lack of technical and financial support poses a dilemma for appraising archivists. Should they reject significant records which, at present, they cannot preserve and use, or should they warehouse material in the hope that technology will soon provide affordable solutions to these archival problems?

• Will the technical quality of the information remain useful after several information transfers? For example, if the original of a magnetic tape recording of oral recollections is very difficult to understand, will the additional distortion produced by repeated information transfers make it unintelligible?

This accession of the David Susskind/Talent Associates library of entertainment films and television programing poses appraisal problems in the selection of production materials used to make a completed film and in the preservation of obsolescent videotapes. (*Robert Granflaten, Courtesy of State Historical Society of Wisconsin*)

(5) graphic records, and (6) combinations of sound and visual records, some in electronic form.

Many archivists feel inadequate and mystified when attempting to appraise these records. This feeling has led some of them either to accept uncritically massive sets of material such as maps, construction plans, and engineering drawings or uncritically reject large files such as negative photographs from newspaper morgues. There is nothing mystical about non-textual records. The basic criteria that have been discussed for determining the value of written records should enable an archivist to determine the informational content and uniqueness of a variety of record formats. There are, however, technical and content considerations that the appraiser must factor into a retention decision.[16]

---

[16] See Trudy Huskamp Peterson, "Archival Principles and Records of the New Technology," *American Archivist* 47 (Fall 1984), 383–93.

• What generation of the record is preferred for preservation? The production and use of sound and visual records often creates two or more generations, whether the record is a simple photographic negative from which a positive print is made or a moving image production involving several generations of sound and visual records. With each successive generation some degradation of the image or sound occurs. Therefore, archivists prefer to accession the original materials and/or the first generation that makes up the final completed production. When it is available, repositories usually accession a later generation as a reference and user copy of the record.

Preferred Accessioning Units for Sound and Visual Records

• black and white still photographs: the camera negative and a first generation print
• color transparencies (slides): the original transparency and one copy
• motion picture film: the original negative or color original with separate sound track, a master positive or duplicate negative and optical sound track, and a projection print or video cassette copy
• video tape: the original recording and one copy
• audio recording discs: the master tape, matrix or stamper, and one disc
• audio tape recordings: the original record and one copy

Draft of New York State Archives Appraisal Manual, 1986

• How dependent is the medium on a particular technology for interpretation and how long will that technology be available? In part, the answer to this question is based on hardware—the machines—that are essential to retrieve the information. For example, the playback equipment for traditional motion pictures, silent or sound, is a low-level technology requiring very little technological support. It is easy to build or reconstruct. Even if this simple equipment is not available, the records can be viewed as still pictures on an image-by-image basis with a loss of motion and sound. In contrast, electronic recording media, even if they prove stable, are very dependent on technological support for information retrieval. Junkyards full of outmoded computer hardware are legion, but machine obsolescence applies to a whole range of modern media. Videotape is a case in point. For twenty-five years, two-inch

The archivist puzzles over data tapes among records to be appraised. Unless there is the necessary hardware, software, and program documentation to read these electronic records, they will be incomprehensible. (*Schoolcraft College.*)

quad videotape was the television broadcasting industry's professional standard. Now it is obsolete. To gain access to the information on these tapes or to transfer the information to a different medium requires sophisticated playback equipment with high-level maintenance requirements and experienced engineers. It is a very expensive process.

• Are the instructions—or documentation—that tell the researcher what information is in the record and how to retrieve it available and adequate? In evaluating machine-dependent records—whether numeric, textual, or graphic—not only must the image be readable but the records must be accompanied by adequate documentation to retrieve and understand the data. For machine-readable records this documentation includes a description of the data elements (i.e., name, address, Social Security number, occupation, and so forth), how the elements are laid out on in the storage medium, and a host of technical information essential for retrieval. Without this information the record is worthless.

In addition to documentation, many electronic records require special software or reformatting to solve the problems of technological dependence, user access, or future information transfers. The New

York State Archives and Records Administration requires the appraiser to analyze all preservation costs, including computer time, contracted services, and staff time. If these costs are prohibitive, the records, with rare exceptions, are rejected.[17]

Appraisal Guidelines for Electronic Records

- Data are at a disaggregate or micro-level rather than in summary or aggregate form.
- Data will be used for statistical analysis or searched on a data element or accessed on a case-by-case basis
- Data can be linked to other machine-readable files.
- Data represent a complete population or universe, or a statistically valid sample.
- Data will be of high interest to researchers in fields where automated techniques are routinely used in research such as sociology, the natural sciences, health and welfare, and political science.
- Retention of information in machine-readable form is cost-effective alternative to the storage of information that would otherwise be preserved on paper or microfilm.
- Retention in machine-readable form significantly improves access, retrieval, and manipulation of the information.
- Names and other personal identifiers can be deleted from machine-readable records to allow researchers access to records that would otherwise be closed.
- Whenever possible, entire automated information systems will be appraised as a single entity.

Draft of New York State Archives Appraisal Manual, 1986

- What related information about the records is available? Parallel documentation may be necessary in appraising sound and visual records. Often these record formats are less well identified than conventional paper records. Therefore, any documentation created by the producer or user of records in these formats regarding their provenance, identity, arrangement, or mode of access should be examined. For example, when appraising professionally

produced still photographs and moving image material, the archivist should look for accompanying caption lists, assignment logs, and film shot logs and indexes. Documentation such as annotated photograph albums and indexes to photograph negatives or slide collections are important in evaluating material created by amateur or family photographers. As with paper records, a collection's value is greatly enhanced by a ready-made descriptive and access system. Without such supporting data, the cost of identifying and arranging the sound or visual records may make their preservation prohibitive.

As the life cycle of new recording formats grows shorter, the problem of technological dependence becomes greater. In this world of technological flux and obsolescence, archivists must act quickly to preserve information. One solution to technological obsolescence is the continual transfer of information to new formats. The costs of such continuing transfers may, however, require that information be appraised anew at each transfer stage.

Important as these technical issues are, the appraiser's larger concern is to develop an awareness and sensitivity to the special informational character of these prolix records and their power to capture secondary information.

Content of the Information. As with traditional textual records, the appraiser also must evaluate the character and quality of the information. How accurate is the visual and sound representation or how significant or rare is the information? are questions any competent appraiser will ask. There are, however, significant characteristics of the information that are not immediately apparent to archivists primarily trained to evaluate paper textual records. In evaluating the information content, the archivist also needs to ask the following:

- Is the secondary or background information in visual records of value? Visual recording media have broad capturing power that results in unexpected or unintended material of great value. Thus the appraiser should give attention not only to the primary information the image contains but to the secondary information as well. A glossy newspaper photograph of an event as pedestrian as an awards banquet may show, in addition to the main event, a historic building interior, the clothing and hairstyles of the diners, and a television film clip may also reveal regional accents and the byplay among the observers at the head table.
- What is the best form of the information? Some events are recorded in every available modality including sound recordings, moving images,

---

[17] Two basic works for appraising electronic records are: Harold Naugler, *The Archival Appraisal of Machine-Readable Records: A RAMP Study with Guidelines* (Paris: UNESCO, 1984), 101 pp.; and Katherine Gavrel, *Conceptual Problems Posed by Electronic Records: A RAMP Study* (Paris: UNESCO, 1990). Still useful though technologically dated is Margaret Hedstrom, *Archives & Manuscripts: Machine-Readable Records* (Chicago: Society of American Archivists, 1984).

still photographs, scripts and transcripts, and written accounts. Given the cost of acquisition and preservation, should all these associated records be accessioned or, for instance, could the still photographs and the transcripts provide adequate documentation?

• How important are variant copies of sound and moving image productions? Because of listening and viewing time constraints, different audiences, and editorial perspective, many of these records are produced in variant editions. While archivists usually prefer to accession the most extensive version, they need to evaluate variant editions, especially where editorial changes slant and or otherwise alter the meaning of the the record's message for a specific audience. Archivists also should be alert to out takes, material created in the course of production but not used in the final version. These out takes, particularly for public affairs and documentary programs, are often a much richer informational resource and have wider historical value than the completed production.

Summary

Appraisal is a process by which the archivist evaluates how well specific records contribute to acquisition policy objectives. The archivist's five basic tools for this evaluation are

• **Functional Analysis.** An examination of who created the record and for what purpose to determine the "evidential" or "informational" significance of records. This analysis is based on the premise that archivists must understand the relationship between the records and the institution's functions if they are to understand the record's significance.

• **Content Analysis.** The archivist must evaluate the significance of the subjects or topics documented in the records and then determine how well the information in the records document those subjects or topics.

• **Context Analysis.** In today's complex information environment, the archivist needs to appraise records in a broader context that examines the comparative relationship between the information in the records and other available information.

• **Use Analysis.** The research value of a record is a function of its usefulness. The archivist needs to know the potential uses that are likely to be made of the records and the physical, legal, and intellectual impediments to access.

• **Cost-Benefit Analysis.** Using this fifth tool (which archivists seldom do), the appraiser weighs the value of the information in a record against the cost of preservation.

These same tools should be used when appraising special classes of record formats, including machine-readable records, still and moving images, sound recordings, and graphic records. In this appraisal, the archivist also examines technical issues of physical stability and durability, technological obsolescence, and information transfer. These nuts-and-bolts issues may be resolved by technological advances and more resources. To deal adequately with the larger intellectual issue of determining informational value, appraisers must become more aware of the special kinds of information found in these media and their power to trap secondary information. They must become as sensitive to the character of this information as they are to that in paper documents.

Selected Readings

General

David Bearman, "Archival Methods," *Archives and Museum Informatics Technical Reports* 3 (Spring 1989), 6–16.

Frank Boles in association with Julia Marks Young, *Archival Appraisal* (New York: Neal-Schuman Publishers, Inc., 1991), 29–74.

Joan K. Haas, Helen Willa Samuels, and Barbara Trippel Simmons, *Appraising the Records of Modern Science and Technology: A Guide* (Boston: MIT, 1985).

Michael A. Lutzker, "Max Weber and the Analysis of Modern Bureaucratic Organizations: Notes Toward a Theory of Appraisal," *American Archivist* 45 (Spring 1982), 119–30.

T. R. Schellenberg, *The Appraisal of Modern Records,* Bulletin of the National Archives No. 8 (Washington, D.C.: National Archives, 1956).

JoAnne Yates, "Internal Communication Systems in American Business Structures: A Framework to Aid Appraisal," *American Archivist* 48 (Spring 1985), 141–58.

Special Classes of Records

Alan Kowlowitz, "Archival Appraisal of Online Information Systems," *Archives and Museum Informatics Technical Reports* 2 (Fall 1988).

Katherine Sue Gavrel, *Conceptual Problems Posed by Electronic Records: A RAMP Study* (Paris: UNESCO, 1990).

Helen P. Harrison, *The Archival Appraisal of Sound Recordings and Related Material* (Paris: UNESCO, 1987).

Margaret Hedstrom, *Archives & Manuscripts: Machine-Readable Records* (Chicago: Society of American Archivists, 1984).

Sam Kula, *The Archival Appraisal of Moving Images: A RAMP Study with Guidelines* (Paris: UNESCO, 1983).

Harold Naugler, *The Archival Appraisal of Machine-Readable Records: A RAMP Study with Guidelines* (Paris: UNESCO, 1984).

Richard Noble, "Considerations for Evaluating Local History Photographs," *Picturescope* 31 (Spring 1984), 17–21.

Rolf L. Schuursma, "Principles of Selection," *Phonographic Bulletin* 9 (1974), 7–8.

―――――, "Principles of Selection in Sound Archives," *Phonographic Bulletin* 11 (1975), 12–19.

Chapter 7

Conducting the Appraisal

The appraisal of records is demanding work. Reaching an informed decision is dependent not only upon the knowledge, skills, insights, and experience appraisers bring to their work but also on the method and thoroughness with which they conduct the examination of the records. What skills and knowledge do archivists need for appraisal work and how are they applied?

The Appraiser's Skills and Knowledge

Analysis and judgment must be informed by the archivist's skills and knowledge, which are general in nature and are usually acquired as part of the archivist's academic training. Other skills and knowledge are repository-specific and usually are acquired in the course of the archivist's employment.

General Skills and Knowledge. Archivists should (1) understand historical research methods and changing patterns of historiography, (2) know the general contours of history, particularly of the modern era, (3) be familiar with trends in institutional development and bureaucratic organizations, and, (4) know the development of records keeping and information technology.

To understand the value of records and what they document and know how to frame historical research questions and identify records that answer those questions, it is important that archivists have training in research methodologies involving the analysis of historical materials. Ideally, the appraiser should be familiar with changing patterns in the interdisciplinary use of historical records.

Archivists should also be informed about the larger historical and societal environment—local, regional, or national—of the record creators. For most American archivists, this means a knowledge of the broad contours of American history and government. Because most appraisal work will involve comparatively recent records, the archivist should be particularly informed about the main currents of twentieth-century life. It is especially important that those appraisers whose mandate is to select records in a larger societal context be broadly knowledgeable about the economic, social, and intellectual life of the nation.

Archivists need to understand the development and functioning of bureaucratic organizations, for these are the principal record creators. This understanding comes from a knowledge of institutional and administrative history. Because of the increasing tendency of law to affect every aspect of life, archivists need to know the law as it relates to the creation, administration, and preservation of records.

Archivists should have a basic knowledge of why records are made and how recordkeeping practices and information systems evolved over time. They need to understand how and why organizations use technology and how changing technology either enhances or decreases the value of the records for creators and secondary users. Why organizations structure records as they do, physically and intellectually, can reveal much about their activities and about their internal and external communications. In the past, some of this knowledge was part of such

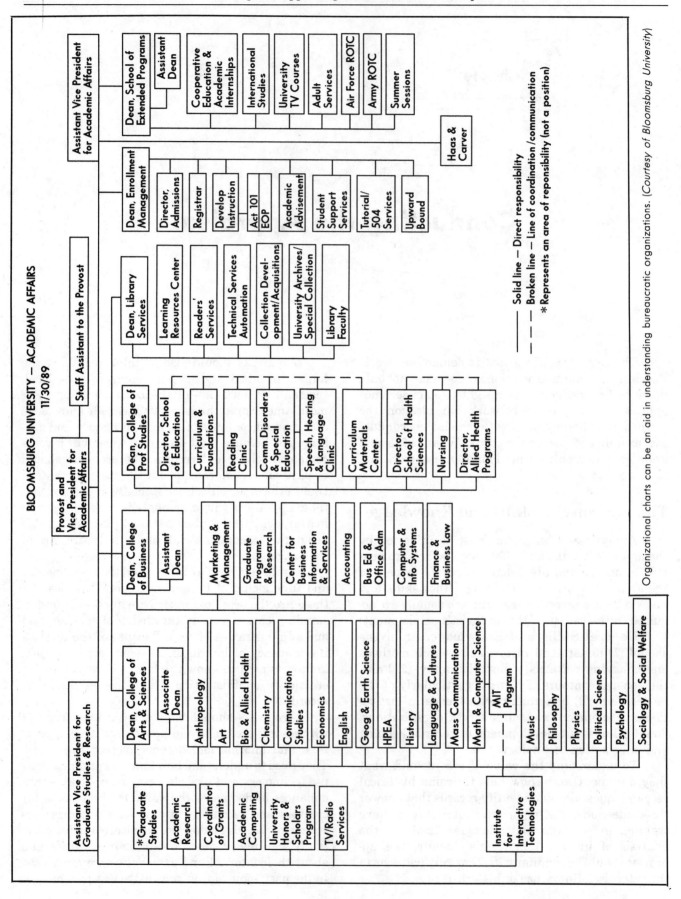

Organizational charts can be an aid in understanding bureaucratic organizations. (*Courtesy of Bloomsburg University*)

auxiliary archival sciences as paleography and diplomatics, the studies of ancient writing and official documents. A modern counterpart is the study of a complex information system, particularly one that manipulates and stores information electronically. Whether the system is a manual or electronic one, the archivist must understand why information was put into it and what it is supposed to do in order to determine what needs to be saved. Without this knowledge the archivist will be at a disadvantage in selecting records in a new information age.

Repository-Specific Knowledge and Skills. The general knowledge and skills acquired by archivists will enable them to develop more easily the specific knowledge they will need in their appraisal work at a particular repository. At this level, the appraiser must have (1) a thorough knowledge of the repository's mandated field of acquisition, its historical background, significant characteristics and development, and current dimensions, (2) a detailed understanding of the entities and functions that create the records, and (3) a knowledge of the records as they relate to each other and to other documentary sources.

For the institutional archivist, the acquisition mandate usually requires not only a knowledge of administrative history, statutes, and regulations but also how the parent organization is structured, what are its primary functions, how and by whom decisions are made, and how information is recorded and transmitted within the organization. This information is usually gained through historical, administrative, and functional analysis of the institution. Appraisers at collecting repositories that accession the records of outside organizations need this same specific knowledge of organizational history, structure, function, and records generation as do institutional archivists.

[The appraiser must] function as an administrative historian and system analyst to understand the origins, relationships, and significance of records.

Maynard J. Brichford, *Archives & Manuscripts: Appraisal & Accessioning*, 1977.

The archival appraiser must also know how an agency's or individual's records relate to each other and to other documentary sources. Institutional archivists who work with a records management program that has already surveyed and scheduled the records have at hand much of the information neces-

sary to understand the interrelationship of an agency's total documentation.

Those collecting archivists seeking to document the broader sinews of American history and life, however, need a larger comparative context. They must know about related bodies of materials, published and unpublished, in parallel subject areas outside their repository, and the acquisition policies of related archival programs.

Reaching a Decision: The Appraisal Process

The appraisal process should be a well-organized activity to gather and analyze information about the records within the framework of collecting policy selection criteria.

Staffing: The Appraisal Specialist. Because of the broad knowledge and analytical skills required to form appraisal judgments, in larger institutions this task is often assigned to more senior and experienced archival staff. Some larger archives have a cadre of appraisers, each responsible for analyzing records related to a particular segment of the acquisitions program. At the National Archives, for example, appraisal duties are broken down and assigned by function, such as legislation or regulation. A team approach, bringing together experts with archival, historical, statistical, legal, and other skills, has been used for complex appraisals, such as that of the Federal Bureau of Investigation case files, while the Penn Central Railroad records appraisal project was an interinstitutional effort.[1] Though many repositories are too small to develop a cadre of appraisal experts, they can organize the appraisal function in ways to develop greater expertise. One approach is to integrate the appraisal function with records processing. The archivist for political papers and records at the State Historical Society of Wisconsin, for example, is responsible for identification, appraisal, arrangement, and description of the records of the state legislators, governors, the congressional delegation, and the major state-level political parties. Whatever the approach, the objective is to build staff expertise in the most efficient manner.

Unit of Analysis. The basic unit of analysis is the records series or, in some instances, a group of closely related series that may form an integrated information system. In collecting archives, the unit of analysis is usually the less well-defined "collection," which may be a single diary or a hundred cubic

---

[1] James Gregory Bradsher, "The FBI Records Appraisal," *The Midwestern Archivist* 13 (1988), 51–66.

After inspecting the records of the Connor Land and Lumber Company stored in a granary in Northern Wisconsin, the archivists have reached a tentative appraisal decision. (*Courtesy of Timothy Ericson and Barbara J. Kaiser*)

feet of organizational records composed of several well-defined series. The series/collection unit usually corresponds to the way most records are created, maintained, and accessioned into the archives.

Steps in Records Analysis. Given the quantity of records most appraisers must examine, they need an efficient evaluation and review process that achieves economy without sacrificing thoroughness. In this process there is a progression of steps: (1) evaluation of available written documentation about the records, followed as necessary by (2) consultation with record creators or custodians, (3) on-site inspection of the records, and (4) assistance from outside experts. This process assumes the appraisal archivist is familiar with the records creator and the functions and activities which produced the records, information often found in such sources as administrative histories, organizational charts and studies, and statutes and administrative rules and regulations.

In government and other institutions where a records analysis and disposition program controls the flow of records to the archival repository, the initial appraisal is often based on information found in the inventory forms and disposition schedules rather than a physical examination of the records themselves. Some archival appraisal authorities, however, require that all schedules be accompanied by a small but representative sample of the records under review, a practice that all archives should observe. Appraisal archivists also should have access to retention schedules for related records of the same administrative unit or of other units pertaining to the same function or activity. The information available at this level of analysis often is sufficient for the archivist to approve a disposition recommendation for many records. The New York State Archives,

for example, estimates that their staff can appraise almost three-fourths of the state's scheduled records based on the information provided through the records management process.[2]

The written documentation about the records is not, however, always adequate. Too often the documentation is ambiguous, misleading, inaccurate, or otherwise deficient. In moving to the second step in appraisal, skilled appraisers know that talking with records creators and custodians can often resolve questions about the records not answered by the documentation. They can provide additional information the appraiser may need about the function of the record and its relationship to other series or sources of information. They can explain a file arrangement or classification system and verify the existence of indexes, registers, or other finding aids essential for accessing the records. Records creators and custodians can not only clarify the administrative, legal, or fiscal purpose of the records, but also offer important insights into the potential of the record for secondary use, frequently providing a corroborative judgment as to the records' long-term value. Records creators and custodians, whether corporate or individual, are the appraiser's friend. While some appraisal questions can be resolved at this level—the New York State archives estimates "another ten to fifteen percent"—some records require an actual examination to make an appraisal decision, particularly unscheduled records and collections.

The third appraisal step is the on-site examination of records. Experienced appraisers know that

---

[2] Draft of the New York State Archives Appraisal Manual, 18.

An appraisal review group discusses report findings prior to making a final retention recommendation. (*Robert Granflaten, Courtesy of State Historical Society of Wisconsin*)

records inventory and scheduling data can be inaccurate or misleading and that many records custodians either have too narrow a view of their records' archival worth or overestimate their historical importance. An on-site examination is imperative when there is doubt regarding the content, arrangement, volume, or physical condition of the record. In the case of unscheduled records, the archivist may have no alternative to conducting an on-site survey. In gathering additional data for appraisal, the archivist also should examine the indexes, inventories, and other finding aids held by the custodian that related to the records.

On-site visits have an important secondary value. They strengthen communication and cooperation between the archivist and the records creator or custodian and educate records personnel about the importance of their records and the value of archival preservation.

Occasionally a fourth appraisal step—consulting with outside experts—is necessary. No matter how knowledgeable archivists are about the areas of their repository's acquisitions mandate, at times they will need expert advice in forming an appraisal decision, particularly on records outside their experience. For many archivists, this means areas such as science and technology, health science and care, and music and arts. Experts may also be needed to clarify the legal ramifications of an accession or to help the archivist in developing a plan for sampling records.

Experts should not be expected, or allowed, to make the appraisal decision. Only the archivist, analyzing a broad range of criteria, should make this decision. Outside consultants can, however, be invaluable in informing a difficult decision. Experts can also provide support for difficult retention decisions in which the records are classified and sensitive, a custodian wants important records destroyed, or a donor wishes unimportant material preserved. Experts often provide the clout needed to support the difficult "political" decisions that affect many appraisals. A consultant's report can help the repository shift the onus for an unpopular decision. Archivists must, however, weigh carefully the propensity of experts to keep more often than destroy records.

The process of evaluating unscheduled records and collections in private hands is similar, though much less linear than the process outlined above. Lead file notes, correspondence, or memoranda of telephone conversations sometimes provide sufficiently reliable information on which to base an evaluation, particularly for smaller collections and records series. As a general rule, however, the appraisal archivist should physically examine records in these categories before reaching a retention decision. To better understand the records, the archivist should request from the custodian/donor information about the collection, its component parts (particularly interrelated personal and business records so often found in intergenerational family collections), its provenance and how the records came into the care of the current custodian, who has legal title to the records, and if there are additional segments of the collection or related records either in or out of archival custody.

In conducting the examination, the field archivist or other appraiser evaluates the records in terms of the criteria discussed in Chapter 6. For large collections, the archivist should take an actual series-by-series inventory. While a series-level inventory may involve several archivists working over a period of time, in the long run it is a great economy. It facilitates weeding out masses of useless records, provides for a more systematic appraisal, and furnishes the archival custodian with vital information that will facilitate the subsequent work of arrangement and description. Many archivists have horror stories regarding the trials and expense in gaining control over acquisitions that were not examined physically or evaluated sufficiently prior to their transfer to the repository.

The Appraisal Report. Disposition recommendations, especially those that may be controversial or involve complex or sensitive records, should be thoroughly documented in a written appraisal report. (See Figure 7-1.) The basic components of the report usually are the following:

- the name of the office that created the records, its major functions and activities, and its position in the administrative hierarchy.

- a description of the records including date, volume, annual accumulation (where relevant), types of records, informational content, and gaps in the record.

- an analysis of whether or not the acquisition falls within the institution's acquisition scope. If it does not, the records will be rejected unless, in the appraiser's judgment, there is some overriding reason an exception should be made. Such exceptions should be rare, compelling, and thoroughly documented and reviewed.

- an analysis of how the records meet various institutional appraisal criteria such as their value in terms of informational content, relationship to other records both in the institution and elsewhere, accessibility, potential use, and cost of retention.

- steps to be taken if the records are accessioned, such as sampling, microfilming, or arranging to a suitable level. If they are to be sampled, the report should include a sampling design.

- the opinion of the appraiser and outside experts on the value of the records.

- the appraiser's retention recommendation and justification in terms of the foregoing.

Reviewing and Approving Appraisal Recommendations. Concern about the finality and future reaction to retention decisions has prompted some repositories to develop a procedure for reviewing appraisal decisions. At the New York State Archives, for example, the appraiser's report is reviewed by peers and approved by the bureau chief in charge of appraisal. If the chief disagrees with the decision, the report is reviewed by the division director and the State Archivist. At the State Historical Society of Wisconsin, all incoming accessions of private records and papers are approved by an appraisal review committee made up of archivists from several program areas. All large repositories should have a review process, perhaps as simple as circulating appraisal reports for comment by selected archivists. The objective of the process is an informed consensus, not unanimity. Collegiality must not permit a lone voice to veto a good decision or prevent

the veto of a bad one and thus render the process ineffective. Whatever the mechanism, a review process makes for a more informed decision. Psychologically, it lightens the appraiser's burden by sharing the responsibility for appraisal decisions. The process also can buffer institutional decisions and protect the administrative leadership from the political fallout from unpopular decisions.

Observations and Caveats

- The goal of the appraiser is to make an informed decision, not an infallible one.
- Today's information-laden world has lessened the value of any single set of records; the documents may be unique but the information is usually not. This lessens the importance of individual appraisal decisions.
- There should be a "definite and compelling justification" for the retention of records.
- Appraisal cannot be done from an archival cookbook with lists of what records are always important, usually important, or occasionally important, because institutional goals and records that help achieve those goals differ. Each appraisal decision is unique.
- While practice will never make perfect, appraisal only improves as appraisers hone their skill on the job.
- Appraisal is only part analysis; for the skilled and creative appraiser, it is also an art.

Summary

Appraisers should bring to their work a broad array of knowledge and skills: some are general and acquired as part of their preparatory academic training, others are repository-specific and gained on the job. Their general background should include familiarity with historical research methods and the uses of records, knowledge of the general contours of the nation's history and its changing historiography, an understanding of institutional development and bureaucratic organizations, and knowledge of the development of recordkeeping and information technology. Within the repository, appraisers must become knowledgeable about its acquisition areas and the institution(s) or individual(s) that created the records it accessions.

The well-organized appraisal process has a progression that the archivist generally will follow: evaluation of available written documentation about the series and, as necessary, consultation with record creators or custodians; on-site inspection of the rec-

Figure 7-1 Appraisal Report

New York State Archives and Records Administration

Appraisal Report No:	90-25
Agency:	Governor's Office of Employee Relations (GOER)
Subdivision:	Child Care Unit (CCU)
Contact:	Sandra Koss, tele. 473-3075
Action Originated:	Submission of Schedule for Office
Title, Date and Volume of Records:	New York State Labor/Management Child Care Advisory Committee Official Files, 1982-current, 6 cubic feet
Location of Records:	Unit office, 1 Commerce Plaza
Condition:	Good

BACKGROUND

The Child Care Unit (CCU) of the Governor's Office of Employee Relations is responsible for the development of New York State employee child care programs. The unit initiates and/or provides assistance in the establishment and expansion of State worksite child care enters under the aegis of not-for-profit corporations, provides seed monies and some operational funding for the centers, assists them in securing other sources of funding, renders general technical assistance to the centers, and monitors their performance in an advisory capacity. The unit also assists the New York State Labor-Management Child Care Advisory Commitee (CCAC) in developing policies related to State Employee child care programs. CCAC also approves funding for child care centers and other associated projects through GOER.

DESCRIPTION

This series consists of 6 cubic feet of standard-sized paper records documenting CCAC monthly meetings. These include minutes, agenda, a copy of the information packet on issues to be discussed, resolution authorizing funding of programs and other activities, and summary fiscal reports from child care centers and various special projects. The series is arranged by meeting date. It is in good condition, presents no access problems, and contains no confidential materials. The series contains very good information on both CCAC and CCU functions and activities, policy development and decisions, individual State Employee child care centers, funding sources for these centers and other CCU programs, and various topics related to child care in general such as educational levels of child care staff, endemically high rates of staff turnover, and implications of evening and sick-child care.

EVALUATION

The wholesale movement of women into the workforce and the proliferation of single parent families has made child care a major social issue during the later 20th century in the United States. Relatively few families across the nation are untouched by the serious problem of how to ensure that their children receive proper care while parents earn a living. According to GOER staff members, the New York State employee child care program is an innovative and groundbreaking answer to this problem for State employees. This series provides excellent primary evidential documentation for this program and will allow policy researchers and historians to evaluate its real effects upon and value to employees and employers alike. The records present no preservation of access problems; they are small in volume, so there are really no difficulties in transfer and accessioning.

RECOMMENDATION

Series CCA001 is archival and should be transferred periodically to the State Archives in accordance with its proposed retention and disposition schedule.

T. Norris, 7/19/90

ords; and, occasionally, use of outside experts. The findings and recommendations, especially for large and/or complex records series or collections or for a decision that is likely to be controversial, should be thoroughly documented in a written appraisal report. Finally, a repository should develop a procedure for reviewing an appraiser's recommendation in order to buttress the decision and buffer the decision-maker.

Selected Readings

Maynard J. Brichford, *Archives & Manuscripts: Appraisal & Accessioning* (Chicago: Society of American Archivists, 1977), 14–18.

Writings on conducting an appraisal are a lacuna in archival literature.

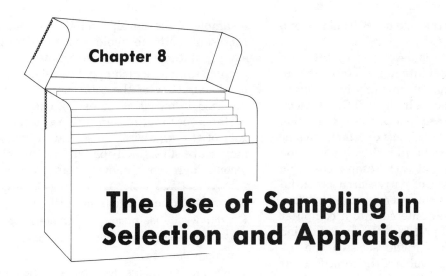

Chapter 8

The Use of Sampling in Selection and Appraisal

Sampling is an underutilized but important tool in archival appraisal kits, especially when dealing with massive series or collections of homogeneous records. Sampling is not new to archivists; in fact, they sample from a larger universe of documentation every time they make a selection. Archivists sample when they choose one set of records over another, when they keep parts of a collection and not others, and when they weed individual folders and items. Appraisal itself is a sampling process, but such sampling is usually qualitative and not based on mathematics. In recent decades, however, archivists have sought to develop statistical and other analytical approaches to reducing the bulk of a potential accession while preserving its research value. In addition to reducing the bulk of an accession, archivists have begun to use sampling in an important new way: to collect and analyze data on which to base the appraisal decision as well as the selective retention plan.

In today's world of archival overabundance, as Dennis P. Affholter points out, it is no longer a question of *whether to use* sampling methods but rather *how to use* them. Therefore, archivists need to understand the fundamental concepts and know the basic applications for sampling archival records and, happily, they do not need to become statistical experts to do so. But, they must make choices about sampling methods and designs as sampling becomes a component of more and more appraisal decisions. While outside experts will usually be needed to provide advice and guidance in constructing a sample, it is the archivist who must determine its purpose. This determination is a basic appraisal question.[1]

Using Statistical Sampling to Inform an Appraisal Decision

Some series of modern institutional records, civil and criminal court case files are a familiar example, are so extensive and voluminous that it is not economically feasible—or even possible—to analyze their content through a file-by-file inspection. Nor can the archivist make an informed appraisal examination simply by inspecting a few files at random. What the archivist needs is a statistical profile of sufficient comprehensiveness and reliability to judge the entire series. One methodology for developing such a profile—computer-assisted sampling for appraisal—was first worked out by Michael S. Hindus and a group of colleagues to appraise some 35,000 cubic feet of records of the Massachusetts Superior Court dating from 1859 to 1959. Since then this pioneering methodology has been used by the National Archives and Records Administration to appraise some 25 million Federal Bureau of Investigation case files, and later, in 1983, 135,000 cubic feet of Department of Justice closed litigation case files, a series

---

[1] Dennis P. Affholter, "Probability Sampling in Archives," presented at the October 1983 meeting of the Society of American Archivists, 3–5, 12. This paper is a lucid and concise introduction for archivists in the use of sampling methods. This manual author has drawn heavily from this fine but, unfortunately, unpublished essay.

that is accumulating at the rate of 5800 cubic feet a year.[2]

A statistical profile is developed by taking a small statistical or probability sample (probable in the sense that the sample is probably an accurate representation of the whole). In the FBI files project, the sample was 18,000 cases out of some 25 million drawn from 214 file classifications of crimes such as bank fraud, espionage, and civil rights. Information about the characteristics of each sample case and the reviewer's evaluation of its research potential and other comments was entered on a standard data collection sheet and then entered into a computer from which a statistical profile of the classification file was generated. This profile assisted the appraiser in determining the value of the records, their relationship to case files in the field offices and legal attachés, and the projected cost of retention.[3]

Sampling for appraisal can be time-consuming and expensive, requiring a great deal of teamwork and consultant expertise. The cost of the FBI files appraisal was estimated at more than $500,000 in 1980s dollars. Sampling to inform an appraisal decision remains, therefore, an exceptional practice.

Using Sampling to Reduce the Bulk of an Accession

A more traditional use of sampling in archives is to reduce the volume of an accession to make the retention of archival records more manageable and affordable. The retention plan for the FBI files, based on the appraisal sample, will reduce the bulk of the original records (39,000 cubic feet) by some 83 percent. In reducing the volume of an accession, the archivist, depending upon the type of records and the purpose for which the sample is being drawn, will use, either singly or in combination, two basic sampling methods. The first, the **probability or statistical** sample, is mathematically based to provide

a sample of measurable reliability that accurately represents both the whole records series and selected sub-populations. The second is a **purposive or judgmental** sample, which may be designed to provide a particular view of the total collection, to preserve itemized information of exceptional historical importance, or to fulfill some other subjective selection goal of the archivist. This kind of sample may or may not be statistically based. In archival usage this second approach is known as archival sampling.[4]

Before designing a sample the archivist needs to ask
- What will be the primary use of the sampled records?
- What sampling technique is most appropriate in supporting that use?
- What resources are available to design and draw the sample?
- What is the trade-off between research use of the records and the resource allocation necessary to carry out the sample? In short, what are the opportunity costs of sampling?

Probability or Statistical Sampling. This sampling approach, also known as mathematical sampling, is designed to "capture all of the major characteristics of a series" while reducing its volume. This method is most suitable for large and homogeneous records series where one file unit or document is as important as any other and no special importance is attached to one file against another.[5] This method, then, is best for sampling large masses of uniform data and files—correctional or welfare case files are examples.

Once archivists have decided what sub-populations should also be accurately represented, they need to determine a statistically valid sample; that is, the percentage of the particular record universe that will accurately represent the whole—perhaps two, five, or ten percent?[6] At this point they may need a statistician's services to determine key measures of reliability which in turn will determine sample size. These measures include (1) the "central tendency" of the records, which is an assessment of their homogeneity, and (2) "dispersion," which is a measure of variability or dispersion from the central ten-

[2] See Michael Stephen Hindus, Theodore M. Hammett, and Barbara M. Hobson, *The Files of the Massachusetts Superior Court, 1859–1959: An Analysis and a Plan for Action* (Boston: G.K. Hall & Co., 1980); *Appraisal of the Records of the Federal Bureau of Investigation: A Report to Hon. Harold H. Greene, United States District Court for the District of Columbia,* submitted by the National Archives and Records Service and the Federal Bureau of Investigation (Washington, D.C.: National Archives and Records Service, 1981), 2 vols.; and National Archives and Records Administration, *Appraisal of Department of Justice Litigation Case Files: Final Report, Washington.* (Washington, D.C.: National Archives and Records Administration, n.d.). For an account of the FBI project see, Bradsher, "The FBI Records Appraisal," 51–66.

[3] Chapter 3 ("Methodology") in *Appraisal of the Records of the FBI.*

[4] Paul Lewinson, "Archival Sampling," *American Archivist* 20 (October 1957), 291–312, is the classic statement on traditional archival sampling.

[5] Frank Boles, "Sampling in Archives," *American Archivist* 44 (Spring 1981), 126.

[6] Male inmates ages 18–25 or two-parent families receiving welfare assistance are examples of sub-populations.

Sampling to reduce the bulk of an accession (particularly large and homogeneous records series such as those shown in the background) is a little used but important selection tool. (*Courtesy of the New York State Archives and Records Administration*)

dency. For this and other statistical information, experts should be consulted.[7] In selecting records for a probability sample the archivist will use either a random or a systematic sampling method.

Random sampling. This method is designed to assure that each case, file, or other unit is as likely to be selected as any other. This method involves assigning each unit in the series a unique identification number, or utilizing existing unique numbers. A random number table is used to select the units that will be in the sample. Random sampling is usually applied to files where the units are filed by some non-random predetermined order such as place of residence or income level. Random selection assures a "purer" sample, unbiased or "unweighted" by the way the record series is organized. But it is cumbersome, time-consuming, and expensive, as the Massachusetts Superior Court records project demonstrated.[8]

Systematic sampling. This is a more straightforward, quicker, and less expensive method that should be used when the file is already organized in random order; that is, there is no importance to the way the files are numbered and/or filed. Examples include documents filed by Social Security number, a consecutive numbering system, or the date a case file was closed (assuming it is a random event).[9] In practice, the archivist draws a systematic sample

by selecting every nth file, such as every tenth or twentieth.

There are some risks in systematic sampling. For example, the file may appear to be in random order, but that order may hide certain trends or patterns over time.[10] Most experts agree, however, that if care is taken in the sample design and selection, the mathematical difference between the two methods is negligible. The important point is that in either type of sample, the archivist should have some assurance that the units are homogeneous and one unit is as likely to be selected as any other.

A probability sample can be drawn in various ways among units in a single records group to represent different aspects of the records. In the FBI files appraisal project, for example, the National Archives staff devised a very small systematic sample of cases from those file classifications with low informational value because this seemed sufficient to provide evidential value in illustrating the nature of investigations. A larger sample was taken of those file classifications with high informational value.

Refining the sample: stratification. In designing a probability sample, archivists may find that a simple selection of random units is too coarse and imprecise. They may need to use more sophisticated designs to insure that some numerically rare characteristics in the records are preserved in the sample, such as a specific geographic area, a small ethnic group, or a certain time period.[11] This process involves the over- or under-sampling (that is, sampling with disproportionately high or low selection rates) of a record according to one or more characteristics or "stratifiers." Surveys of the United States population, for example, often draw stratified samples by income, intentionally over-sampling the poor and the rich because they are less numerous than the middle class.[12] To take a second example, the Massachusetts Superior Court Records project compensated for the small number of early court cases by drawing a stratified sample with a much higher percentage of files preserved for those years. Taking a stratified sample is particularly important where a subgroup is likely to be studied separately.

The Purposive or Judgmental Sample. There are many situations in which statistical reliability is unnecessary, and where a non-mathematical representation of records documenting an activity is preferable. The archivist needs to use special

---

[7] Affholter, "Probability Sampling in Archives," 21 ff. For an introduction to sample design, see Bill Williams, *A Sampler on Sampling* (New York: John Wiley and Sons, 1978).

[8] David R. Kepley, "Sampling in Archives: A Review," *American Archivist* 47 (Summer 1984), 239–40.

[9] Affholter, "Probability Sampling in Archives," 18.

[10] See Boles, "Sampling in Archives," 128, for a brief note on these "hidden regularizers."

[11] Kepley, "Sampling in Archives: A Review," 241.

[12] Affholter, "Probability Sampling in Archives," 18.

National Archives' Federal Bureau of Investigation Records Appraisal Task Force members drafting their appraisal report, October 1981. (*Courtesy of Greg Bradsher, Bradsher Collection*)

selection methods that will save either particular records of exceptional historical importance or material that is illustrative of a norm but does not have mathematically measured reliability. In a purposive sample, the goals of selection are determined by the selector's judgment, not by some mathematical formula. Variously called purposive, judgmental, selective, or subjective sampling, it is the method most familiar to and used by archivists.

Itemized selection of exceptional material. A properly conducted probability sample from the FBI files dealing with violations of the Volstead Act would give us a valid statistical profile of bootleggers, but a biographer of Alphonso Capone surely would want Scarface Al's file, which would have a good chance of being destroyed in a probability sample. To capture **significant** and **atypical** information in the FBI case files, the National Archives staff, with the assistance of scholars around the nation, identified for preservation about 4,000 so-called "exceptional cases" which contained information of unusual historical importance. The criteria for selecting atypical records of unusual significance should be spelled out as precisely as possible. Based on the examination of the FBI cases, for example, the project staff developed a list of twelve criteria to assist in the future selection of exceptional files. These criteria included cases accepted by the Supreme Court that involved FBI investigative activities, the ten most wanted criminals, organizations on the Attorney General's list of subversive organizations, and all files of twenty of more sections. More re-

cently the federal government has selected records of exceptional historical interests to document ethnic groups and minorities. The National Archives and Records Administration's Department of Justice litigation case files project staff has recommended the retention of "virtually all civil rights case files" including those "relating to peonage and Indian rights."

The staff of the Massachusetts Superior Court records project had already addressed this issue of quantifying historical interest in order to make the selection process less time-consuming and more routine. They developed a method based on a remarkably simple concept called the "fat file" theory. In appraising one hundred years of trial court records the staff found that the most reliable indicator of a case's research value was its size; i.e., that thick files more likely are about exceptional cases than thin ones. In this case "thick" was defined as at least one and one-half to two inches, depending upon the time period. The theory may not be of universal applicability, but in modified form it was also used in the FBI files project, which recommended retaining all those cases consisting of more than one folder. The appraisal examination of federal Justice Department litigation case files also supported this theory.[13] An irony of the fat file theory, however, is that it adds to the bulk of records archivists are trying to reduce.

In addition to size there are probably other easily identified predictors of historical importance. For example, litigation cases heard on appeal, as common sense would suggest and the Massachusetts project verified, are much higher in historical importance than cases closed without an appeal. In developing alternatives for the selective retention of records, archivists need to hypothesize and test such predictors.

Other purposive selection designs. Most purposive samples are not designed to capture the exceptional and atypical but to select material that is illustrative or representative, though not statistically valid. Here, archivists are looking for a selection of records that will document a routine or a recurring activity. For example, they may take a periodic selection of the complaint files from a state office of consumer protection and citizen advocacy to document the complaint resolution process. While an illustrative sample can have statistical validity, the purpose

---

[13] Hindus, *The Files of the Massachusetts Superior Court*, 80–81; *Appraisal of Department of Justice Litigation Case Files*, 2, 25–28.

of such a sample and a probability design are different. The archivist may keep the records of a single field office as representative of bureaucratic activity at that level. The Massachusetts Superior Court records project recommended the complete retention of the files of one major county for records linkage purposes; that is, to link these records to such other basic historical sources as vital records and census data.

Sometimes the archivist will need to use a combination of sampling approaches and applications to achieve various goals: probability sampling to reduce bulk while preserving the research value of the records; stratified sampling to better represent under-represented or important characteristics of the series; purposive sampling to preserve historically important itemized information or illustrate a process; and total retention of a selected segment of the record for record linkage and other purposes.[14] Furthermore, the sampling process must be meticulously documented. It is imperative that the finding aid to any sampled series have precise and detailed information, mathematical and otherwise, on the sample design and how it was drawn, and a detailed description of the original universe of records, including what was not retained.

Observations and Caveats

- Archival appraisers cannot justify destroying important data because of its bulk without first analyzing the applicability and cost of sampling for both appraisal and selection.
- Sampling can be made comprehensible and useful to archivists. Arcane as mathematical sampling may first appear, archivists are capable of mastering the basic knowledge required to work effectively with statistical consultants.
- The criteria for making sampling choices should be based on archival need, not statistical expertise. Because appraisers know the archival significance of a records series they should make basic decisions about what to save and which sampling method is most appropriate. Consultants assist the

archivist in implementing the appraisal decision. They should not dictate that decision.

- The archivist must do a thorough analysis of what purposes the sampled records should serve before calling in the statistical experts.
- Different sampling methods have different strengths and weaknesses. It is essential that the archivist know what they are and apply the appropriate method. For large collections or records series with varied content, the archivist may need to use a combination of sampling methods.
- Identifying records of exceptional historical interest, even with improved selection tools, takes more time and expertise than most archival repositories can marshal.
- There is no sample that will be of universal applicability for future research. Therefore, the analysis of records to be sampled must be unusually thorough. Nevertheless, the fact that sampling records for certain purposes may impair its usefulness for others should not deter the archivist from selecting a sampling design. Above all, archivists should not worry once the decision is made. Remember, all appraisal is but sampling the larger universe of records; all appraisal is a "calculated risk."[15]

Selected Readings

Frank Boles, "Sampling in Archives," *American Archivist* 44 (Spring 1981), 125–30.

James Gregory Bradsher, "The FBI Records Appraisal," *Midwestern Archivist* 13 (1988), 51–66.

Felix Hall, *The Use of Sampling Techniques in the Retention of Records: A RAMP Study with Guidelines* (Paris: UNESCO, 1981).

Michael Stephen Hindus, et al., *The Files of the Massachusetts Superior Court, 1859-1959: An Analysis and a Plan for Action* (Boston: G. K. Hall and Co., 1980) 3–16.

David R. Kepley, "Sampling in Archives: A Review," *American Archivist* 47 (Summer 1984), 237–42.

Paul Lewinson, "Archival Sampling," *American Archivist* 20 (October 1957), 291–312.

---

[14] Affholter, "Probability Sampling in Archives," 11.

[15] Boles, "Sampling in Archives," 125.

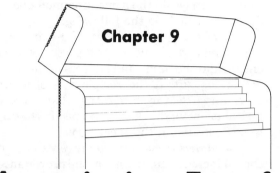

Chapter 9

Accessioning: Transferring Records to the Custody of the Archival Repository

The final step in the selection process is taking physical, and, in most cases, legal custody of the records. In so doing, the archivist accepts responsibility for the records from the previous custodian or the donor. At the accessioning stage the archivist will take preliminary steps to physically store and preserve the records and provide for their retrieval. Though the accessioning process appears simple, the wise archivist will give particular attention to the legal and custodial details. Because accessioning is also the beginning of the arrangement and description process, the reader will find a much fuller account of establishing initial physical and descriptive control in *Arranging and Describing Archives and Manuscripts* (Archival Fundamental Series). This chapter concentrates on the jurisdictional and legal transfer of acquisitions and the physical aspects of getting the records to the archival receiving dock.

The Transfer of Jurisdictional and/or Legal Custody

While the transfer of legal ownership and physical custody of records may occur simultaneously, archivists usually establish their rights to and responsibilities for records before taking physical possession of them. For most governmental and other institutional archives, so-called "legal" transfer involves a change of custody or jurisdiction—not a transfer of legal title—from the original creator or current custodian to the archival authority which assumes responsibility for safekeeping of, and access to, the records. In many cases, ownership remains with the parent institution. On the other hand, when

a repository accepts a privately owned collection, whether institutional records or personal papers, it usually involves a transfer of legal title to the property, although occasionally the material is accepted on deposit.[1]

Transfer by Authorized Disposal Schedules. In institutions with records management programs, the disposal schedule is the primary instrument authorizing and regulating the transfer of records to archival custody. For the institutional repository, the disposal schedule is the basis of an active acquisition program, assuring the repository a steady flow of accessions. If the schedules are adhered to, archivists will know the quantity of records the repository will be receiving during any given period and, thus, they can more accurately plan and better organize their accessioning activities.

Unscheduled Transfers. While the use of disposition schedules to regulate the custodial transfer of current records can be expected to encompass more and more records, there are many accessions, particularly of older records, that are not scheduled. These "irregular" accessions can turn up at any time and in any place. Even in institutions with excellent scheduling programs, the archivist has to contend with the transfer of obsolete records that turn up in the course of a housecleaning or are otherwise accidentally discovered. Not all unscheduled transfers are fortuitous. In many states, for example,

---

[1] For a detailed discussion of the legal aspects of accessioning, the standard work is Gary M. Peterson and Trudy Huskamp Peterson, *Archives & Manuscripts: Law* (Chicago: Society of American Archivists, 1985), 20–38.

county or municipal government officials are not required to schedule their records but must notify the state archival authorities of any pending disposition and offer the records to the archives.

The repository's custodial rights to and responsibilities for these unscheduled records must be thoroughly documented. Instruments used for transferring such records may include an inventory listing of records, duly authorized and signed, or an exchange of memoranda spelling out the statutory or other bases for the change of custody. Where there is an actual transfer of title to the records, such as from a county court to the state archives, the archivist should receive a signed release of title to the records.

Documenting Donations: Transfer by Deed of Gift. Once potential donors have made a decision to place materials in the archives and an appraisal report recommending acceptance has been approved, the field agent is ready to begin the final phase of the selection process: completing the legal and physical transfer of the donation to the archival institution. Legal title to donated records is customarily conveyed by a deed of gift, one of the most important legal documents the archivist will ever sign. The purpose of the document is to transfer a clear title from the creator or other rightful owners to the repository. The deed of gift also spells out the conditions governing the acquisition of the collection, how it is to be preserved, and the terms of access to the records. Some deeds of gift are nothing more than an exchange of letters between the parties indicating an offer and acceptance, as was the case of the since-disputed gift of the Martin Luther King papers to Boston University.[2] Most repositories with an active collecting program, however, use a standardized form. If well-designed, it can be easily modified to deal with most common legal contingencies of transfer. For more complex agreements, archivists should tailor a deed to the specific requirements of the donor and repository. Whether using a standard or customized deed of gift, the archivist should have the document reviewed and approved by the repository's legal counsel. Major donors will often have

their attorneys do the same. Common elements of a deed of gift include the following:

• *The donor and donee.* These are the donor's name and address, whether a person or a corporate entity, and the name and address of the legal recipient of the gift. If the recipient is other than the repository (e.g., the state rather than the state's historical agency), the deed may specify that the gift is to be deposited in the repository.

• *Material conveyed to the repository.* The deed should include a brief note on the provenance as well as the scope and content of the collection, approximate dates covered by the documents, and the physical volume of the accession. For large collections in good organizational order, the donor or the archivist may prepare and attach an inventory to the deed of gift.

• *Rights conveyed to the repository.* The deed should provide not only for the transfer of tangible property rights but, if possible, any copyright the donor may have in the collection. The donor will often hold copyright to other documents already in the repository's collections, particularly where the program has a sharply focused sphere of collecting. The deed of gift should ask donors to assign these— and any future—rights to the archives as well. Where a copyright, particularly one that produces royalty payments to the owner, is not immediately assigned to the repository, the deed should make provision for eventual transfer.

• *Restrictions on access.* While archivists generally prefer acquisitions to be as free of access restrictions as possible, they are sometimes necessary to satisfy a donor's concerns about sensitive material. Equally important, the archivist has an ethical responsibility to inform the donor when restrictions are needed to protect personal privacy or for other legal reasons. Restrictions on access should be explicit and easy to enforce. Where possible, the archivist should limit restrictions only to those materials that can be identified as sensitive. Many archivists will recommend a temporary restriction until the collection is processed and those documents that require further restriction can be more precisely identified. Unreasonable restrictions should be avoided and all restrictions should have an expiration date. Access to governmental and other corporate records is usually governed by statute or institutional polices and directives.

• *Disposition of unwanted material.* Most collections contain material unwanted by the repository—unrelated published material, artifacts, or records of insufficient value. Donor agreements often

---

[2] King, in a July 16, 1964 letter, gave 83,000 of his documents, 1956–1961, to Boston University. Coretta Scott King claimed her husband only meant for the university to be a "repository for a collection of his early papers." University officials said the papers were a gift from Dr. King. *Christian Science Monitor,* February 9, 1988. On January 13, 1992, a Massachusetts state judge ruled that the University and Mrs. King must go to trial to determine who has lawful rights to the documents; *New York Times,* January 14, 1992.

empower the repository to dispose of such materials as it sees fit. Some donors stipulated that discarded materials be returned to them or disposed of in some other manner. The deed should also specify if items of value unrelated to the collection—stamps and coins, for example—are to be returned to the donor or disposed of to the repository's advantage. When a deed transfers property unencumbered to a repository, the institution is legally free to dispose of the material as it sees fit. As a general rule, however, most deeds should state that at some time in the future the collection may be transferred to some more durable and compact medium such as microfilm or some form of electronic storage and the originals disposed of, or that the entire collection may be deaccessioned, without copying, in accord with the repository's deaccessioning policy. The deed should specify what actions the repository is to take if the donation is deaccessioned such as returning it to the donor or the donor's heirs.

• *Special provisions for administering the acquisition.* The deed, for example, should specify the amount and type of reference service the repository will provide to the donor, including the temporary loan or copying of material. These services are often vitally important to corporate donors. The deed, therefore, should precisely define the services the repository will provide and indicate who will pay what costs. The deed should also specify if the repository has agreed to process the collection by a certain date or promised any other special treatment. For example, the agreement should specify if parts of the collection, such as an old diary or some intimate family letters, are to be photocopied and returned.

• *Provision for future accessions.* Where it is evident that there will be future additions to the original donation, the initial deed of gift should make provision for this. The deed should state that the terms of the original gift shall apply to subsequent additions unless they require some special amendment to the initial document.

Some donors prefer to retain possession of their papers until their death, yet provide for eventual transfer. To assure that their wishes are carried out, donors should be encouraged to draw up a codicil to their will in consultation with both their attorney and the field archivist. The codicil should contain the same stipulations that would have been included had the donor executed a deed of gift.[3]

Deposit Agreements. While repositories prefer outright donation, a deposit agreement can be a useful adjunct in acquiring and preserving records, particularly of active organizations whose corporate owners are not willing or able to relinquish title. Philip P. Mason argues that on-going organizations, such as labor unions, should not abrogate title to their archives but place them in a host repository on deposit, an arrangement which he believes benefits both the donor and the repository. The right to abrogate the agreement, he believes, disciplines both parties to fulfill their responsibilities while the on-going nature of the agreement assures a close and continuing relationship with the donor. Archivists should be guarded, however, in their use of deposit agreements so that they do not end up providing would-be donors with unreimbursed storage, processing, and reference services, only to have the records withdrawn.

Deposits should be governed by a meticulously drafted legal instrument similar to a deed of gift. The document should specify the nature of deposit, whether it is (1) semi-permanent (often called "permanent"): material can only be withdrawn for specific reasons; (2) timed, that is, after a specified time period the agreement either terminates or becomes a deed of gift; or (3) open-ended: the agreement is in effect until terminated by either party. Because a deposit agreement should be, in effect, a statement of intent to donate, open-ended agreements should be a contract of last resort. If the depositor is an individual, the agreement should provide for the transfer of title in case of death. Agreements should also spell out what services will be performed by the repository, the responsibilities of the depositor, such as cost sharing, and what liabilities, if any, the repository assumes in taking custody of the records. Finally, the agreement should stipulate that if the depositor unilaterally withdraws the collection, he will reimburse the repository for all costs including transfer, supplies and services, and storage incurred in managing the records. Because of the potential problems in accepting records on deposit, many repositories have a blanket prohibition on the practice.[4]

Agreements Covering the Loan of Records for Photocopying. The purpose of these agreements is fundamentally the same as a deed of gift, and repositories often use the same basic form

---

[3] The authoritative statements on preparing instruments of gift are Trudy Huskamp Peterson, "The Gift and the Deed," *American Archivist* 42 (January 1979), 61–66; and Peterson and Peterson, *Archives & Manuscripts: Law,* 24–27.

[4] See Dennis F. Walle, "The Deposit Agreement in Archival Collection Development," *The Midwestern Archivist* 10 (1985), 117–27.

for both documents. In addition to such matters as copyright and restrictions, the agreement should specify the time frame in which the work will be completed, whether the donor is to receive a copy of the duplicated material (often on microfilm), whether the donor is to reimburse the repository for all or part of the reproduction costs, and who has liability for the collection while it is in the archives' custody.

The deed of gift and other agreements should be reviewed by the repository's legal counsel and signed by all parties to the agreement. No matter how records come into the custody of the archives, the archivist must have written documentation that establishes the repository's custodial rights or legal title to the records. Legal disputes and litigation between donors and repositories are uncommon, but they do occur. In some instances, repositories have had to relinquish custody of collections because they could not establish legal title. Careful attention to the legal aspects of archival custody can save later expense and misunderstanding. These agreements are also part of the basic documentation for subsequent control of the collection and should be incorporated into the collection case file.

Model Deed of Gift or Deposit Agreement for the Donation or Deposit of Historical Materials in an Archives

In tailoring a deed of gift or deposit agreement to the needs of their repository and donors, archivists should first examine the examples found in *Archives and Manuscripts: Law*, pages 28 through 34. These models are designed to be used in whole or in part, as appropriate, and include alternative paragraphs that can be substituted at the donor's requests for other paragraphs in the body of the model documents.

Taking Physical and Administrative Custody

When a repository takes jurisdictional custody of or legal title to an accession, it also accepts responsibility for the care of the records. This requires the archivist to take physical custody in a timely fashion, provide initial access to the records, and preserve them until such time as they are fully arranged and described. To do this, archivists must provide a basic

level of control, for both the physical records themselves and the information about them.[5]

Initial Control of Scheduled Records. The records management program should do much of the work needed to establish initial control of the records before they reach the archival loading dock. Where such a program exists, accessioning should be a smooth and largely routine process. The physical transfer of records is generally controlled by either an inventory or transmittal list, which provides a box-listing, and in some instances a folder-listing for the accession. These lists, along with the descriptive information found in the record schedules, should give the archivists the information they need to establish preliminary descriptive control. The repository can make the records immediately accessible by transposing the information in the transmittal list and on the boxes to its own notational and locational systems. Accessioning under these ideal conditions involves little more than checking the records against the transmittal list, doing basic record-keeping and data entry, and finding a place to shelve the records. (See Figure 9-1.)

The sooner non-current records are transferred to the archives, the more likely their file order will be intact and the better their state of preservation. Unfortunately, many offices ignore a schedule's directives and keep records that should be transferred to archival custody. Therefore, archivists must continuously monitor compliance with approved disposition schedules, requisitioning records from their custodians where necessary. Monitoring is imperative in the case of fragile or ephemeral records such as the archival master microfilm copy, electronic records and their accompanying software and documentation, and sound and visual records of all sorts. Archivists should keep a tickler file, preferably an automated one, to remind them of critical dates.

Unscheduled Acquisitions. While records scheduling increasingly provides records series with a passport to the archives, most archival accessions, particularly those of collecting institutions, continue to arrive in less regular ways. The work of physically transferring unscheduled accessions is facilitated or handicapped by the extent and quality of pre-accession work. Where the records have been inventoried and appraised, and those of archival value identified and segregated, transfer involves little more than making sure the records are properly packed, the

---

[5] See Chapter 4 in Miller, *Arranging and Describing Archives and Manuscripts* for a more detailed discussion of activities at the accessioning stage.

Figure 9-1   Records Transmittal Inventory Form

UNIVERSITY OF WISCONSIN—MADISON **RECORDS TRANSMITTAL/INVENTORY** Form No. UW A-1 PAGE __1__ OF __3__	**INSTRUCTIONS:** Completion of this form is required prior to transfer of records to the University Archives or campus records center facility. A completed form should accompany records to be transmitted. *Consult campus records manual for instructions. Phone 262-3290 for assistance.*

1. Name of Transmitting Office University of Wisconsin Centers	*For Archives Use Only*	
2. Address of Transmitting Office 150 E. Gilman Street, Madison, Wisconsin 53708-8680	**Accession Number** 92/3	
3. Person Preparing Statement Lyn Reigstad	4. Telephone 608/262-2578	**Date Received** *Mo./Day/Yr.* *1/12/92*
5. Volume 1.0 Cubic Feet	6. RDA Number 285R/00027	**Received By** DC
7. Title/Date of Records Minority/Disadvantaged Programs	**Location** 7-R-7	

8. Special Conditions *If records being transmitted are other than hard copy documents, indicate storage medium. If records are confidential, indicate access restrictions.*

	RECORDS INVENTORY	
Box/ Container No.	Folder/ Item No.	Title of Folder/Item
1	1	UWCS Annual Report on Progress & Achievement of Goals & Plans to Improve Services For American & Racial Ethnic Minority Students for 1978–79.
	2	Regent M/D Evaluation Due 4/1/84
	3	UWCS 1979–80 Progress & Achievement of Goals for American Racial & Ethnic Minority Students
	4	M/D Annual Report 1982–83
	5	M/D Annual Report 1983/84
	6	Annual Report to Regents on Minority Enrollment/Graduation Goals 1986.
	7	UWS Central Admin Analysis Paper on Academic Support Services for Minority/Disadvantaged Students AP-7 6/18/73
	8	Conference on Teaching Offenders 3/12–13/87
	9	M/D In-Service Info 1980
	10	M/D Allocation Distribution April–Sept. 1981
	11	UW Systemwide Conference, May 16–17, 1979
	12	Minority Recruitment Retention Retreat (5–20/21–82) Workshop (5/27–28/82)
	13	PREP Correspondence 1985–86
		Use additional sheets if necessary

Figure 9-2a   Internal Transfer Form

Evangelical Lutheran Church in America Archives

Extension: 2818

INTERNAL TRANSFER FORM

1. Name of church: __Evangelical Lutheran Church in America (ELCA)__

2. Name of unit: __Commission for Multicultural Ministries (CMM)__

3. Name of sub-unit (department), if any: _____

4. Record Series Title: __AAAHNA Advisory Committees__

5. Name of Person(s): _____

6. Title of Persons(s): _____

7. Inclusive dates: __1988–1991 (These Committees no longer exist)__

8. Amount: _____ Box ____1____ or ____2____

9. <u>Brief Description</u>:

    Asian Advisory Committee Meeting materials
(correspondence, minutes etc.)

    African American Advisory Committee Meeting materials
(correspondence, minutes etc.)

    Hispanic Advisory Committee Meeting materials (minutes
only)

10. <u>Comments</u>:

    WITH THE RECONFIGURATION OF THE ELCA THE ASIAN, AFRICAN
AMERICAN, HISPANIC, AND NATIVE AMERICAN (AAAHNA) ADVISORY
COMMITTEES NO LONGER <u>EXIST</u>. THESE RECORDS CONTAIN
INFORMATION FROM 1988 TO 1991.

11. <u>Individual Responsible for Transfer</u>:

    Name: __Tina Marie Brown__

    Unit: __Commission for Multicultural Ministries (CMM)__

    Title: __Senior Secretary__

    Extension: __2842__

12. Date of Transfer: __May 8, 1992__

---

boxes correctly identified and marked in sequential order, and the information entered on a transmittal list. Much of this work can be done by clerical staff, but it is usually advisable for the archivist to oversee personally the transfer of large or complex accessions. When accessions arrive in good order, the work of establishing initial control should involve little more work than that associated with scheduled records. (See Figure 9-2.)

More familiar to many archivists, particularly those at collecting institutions, are what might aptly be called "disorderly" accessions. These are the acquisitions that have been haphazardly stored over time in attics, vaults, barns, basements, warehouses, and closets. Most likely their creators or custodians, whether corporate or individual, never considered that the records might be placed in an archival repository. The circumstances of acquisition may have precluded a systematic survey and comprehensive, in-depth appraisal of the records prior to their legal transfer. As a result, much chaff is likely to be shipped along with the wheat. In such cases, it is

Figure 9-2b   Internal Transfer Form (Instructions)

Evangelical Lutheran Church in America Archives

How to Use Internal Transfer Form

The form at left is to be used whenever records from ELCA units are to be transferred directly to the archives. A decision on when materials should be transferred to the archives should be made by a unit in consultation with the Chief Archivist. Extra copies of this form are available from the Executive Assistant for Records Management, the Office of the Secretary, or the archives. Also, a copy of this form will be part of the ELCA Records Management Manual and may be photocopied. This form should not be used for serial publications, such as newsletters and minutes, that are sent to the archives on a regular basis.

Please complete the form as follows:

1. Name of church: For some time, older records will be from either ELCA or one of its predecessors or from LCUSA or a related agency. Please list all churches involved, if materials from several places are now filed together.

2. Name of Unit: Office, Board, Division, Commission, etc. of ELCA or predecessor church.

3. Name of sub-unit (department): Not all units are subdivided, but this information should be provided for units that are subdivided.

4. Records Series Title: Files in an office are usually organized in groups according to a particular function in that office. A records series title represents a familiar title assigned to a file, for retrieval purposes. Examples might be: General Subject Files, Synod Correspondence, Quarterly Reports, etc.

5. Name of Person(s): The person or persons who were directly responsible for creating and/or receiving the correspondence, reports, etc. in this records series.

6. Title of Person(s): The title of the position held by the records creator, such as: Executive Director, Administrative Assistant, etc.

7. Inclusive dates: As well as can be determined, list the dates so as to indicate the oldest and most recent materials included.

8. Amount and Box Number: Please indicate the number of boxes being sent, then photocopy the form that number of times, in order to include a copy in each box, indicating: Box 1 of (total); Box 2 of (total); etc.

9. Brief Description: Anything else that would provide archives staff with details on the nature of the records that is not evident in #1–8 above. Is the material in chronological or alphabetical order; type of materials, such as financial or legal; audio visual; bound volumes, etc; or a note on physical condition. Any descriptive information that already exists, such as folder title listings, indexes, etc., should be attached or sent with the form.

10. Comments: Note here anything out of the ordinary. This may include a note on whether material is confidential.

11. Individual Responsible for Transfer: The person responsible for contacting the archives and arranging for boxing of materials and completing this form.

12. Date of Transfer: Please indicate the date the form is completed.

For further information, please call the archives, extension 2818.

EW/pms/01-27-89

Three vans moved 950 cubic feet of records of the International Harvester Corporation's Farm Implement Division to a new home. (*Robert Granflaten, Courtesy of State Historical Society of Wisconsin*)

The work done by personnel from Navistar and the new repository prior to shipment assured a smooth transfer and expedited initial physical and intellectual control. (*Robert Granflaten, State Historical Society of Wisconsin.*)

imperative that an experienced archivist supervise the sorting, inventorying, packing, and shipping of the records. During this process the custodian or donor may also provide additional information about the provenance and structure of the accession that will prove invaluable in managing the collection. Conversely, archival horror stories abound of donors and/or shippers who, by careless packing, have vastly complicated archival control of the records. Further, some repositories in failing to oversee this process have paid princely sums for the shipment of what turned out to be largely extraneous materials. In the transfer of large "disorderly" accessions, professional on-site supervision and preparation is a great archival economy.

Shipping Arrangements

For many repositories, the physical moving of the records to the repository is a matter of small

moment. Many acquisitions involve nothing more than an intrainstitutional move of records from an office or records center to the archives, or an archivist packing and transporting a modest-sized collection as part of field activity. But major acquisitions, especially those from a great distance, usually must be transported by commercial shippers, a costly proposition. In a more competitive and affluent past, many repositories were only too willing to pay these costs as an inducement to the donor. Increasingly, however, repositories ask donors, particularly institutional ones, to defray these expenses at least in part. Collecting institutions should be able to recommend to donors those shipping companies that have handled such transfers in a satisfactory manner.

Requisitioning Records

Many offices retain historically important records long after their primary administrative usefulness has ceased. These records may become endangered by careless storage in a destructive environment. Many state public records laws empower the state's archival authority to requisition older records unduly retained in an administrative office, or any record in an endangered status. Archivists working in other institutional settings should proceed in a parallel manner to accession such records and, where appropriate, point out to prospective donors the dangers in delaying transfer of important and fragile records to the archives.

Controlling Information about Accessions

The identification, appraisal, and accessioning process should generate basic information about the structure, composition, and content of the records as a foundation for the subsequent work of arrangement and description. For example, those state archives that now enter series level data from records schedules into the RLIN database have a usable description of a records series before it is accessioned. With a few simple modifications of existing scheduling and transmittal information, the archivist will have basic physical and descriptive information needed to control the records. Donor lead and case file data should provide similar descriptive information for private records and papers. As more and more repositories automate record control information, data from these sources should be integrated into a system that will provide needed "process control" information for many subsequent archival functions ranging from storage, preservation, and

Figure 9-3 RLIN Entry for a State Government Record Series

Note: This entry was compiled from an office-specific records schedule and updated (see boldface type) at the time of accessioning.

1)   WIHV91-A684

   ID:WIHV91-A684   RTYP:d   ST:p   MS: EL:z   AD: 05-21-91
   CC:9554   BLT:bc   DCF:a   CSC:d   MOD: PROC: UD: 07-12-91
   PP:wiu   L:eng   PC:i   PD:1946/9999   REP:?
   MMD: OR: POL: DM: RR: COL: EML: GEN: BSE:

  035   **(WHi)820**
  035   (WHi)822
  040   WHi#cWHi#eappm
  052   4120
  110 1   Wisconsin.#bDept. of Natural Resources.#bDivision of Enforcement.
  245 00   Law enforcement investigation case files - Prosecutions,#f1946-<ongoing
  300   **15.0#fc.f.**
   351   #bNumerical and thereunder chronological.
  520   Records created in response to Ch. 29, Wis. Stats., regarding illegal use of fish and game. This series includes records documenting serious violations, investigation charges, and findings; and copies of legal proceedings, testimony, briefs, etc. Records also document multi-state and federal undercover "sting" operations, such as the Operation Gillnet, case and Mesabi case.
  584   Accumulation: 1.0 c.f./year.
  506   Restricted: Access to these records is resricted under Section 905.09, Wis. Stats. Researchers wishing to use these records should directly contact the Chief of Special Investigations Bureau of the Division of Enforcement, DNR.
  580   In record WIHV86-A901 may be found a history of the agency which created these records.
  650 0   Fishery law and legislation#zWisconsin.
  650 0   Game-laws#zWisconsin.
  655 7   State government records.#2aat
  690 4   Scheduled.
  773 1   #w(CStRLIN)WIHV86-A901
  851   Current records are in the office of origin; semi-current records may be in the State Records Center.
  851   #3Non-current records are at the#aState Historical Society of Wisconsin.#bArchives Division.#c816 State Street, Madison, Wis. 53706.
  LDB   Retention and disposition: Retain for#b15 years after closed and#e transfer to the State Archives.

Courtesy of the State Historical Society of Wisconsin

statistical accounting to arrangement, description, and access. (See Figure 9-3.)

Summary

   • The last step in the selection process is to take physical and, in most cases, legal custody of the records. By this act the archivist accepts responsibility for the records from the previous custodian or the donor for the records.

   • In those institutions with records management programs, the records disposal schedule is the primary instrument authorizing and regulating the transfer of records to archival custody.

   • For donated records, legal title is usually conveyed by a deed of gift which should transfer a clear title to the repository and spell out the conditions governing the acquisition and administration of the records.

   • The deed of gift and other agreements should be reviewed by the repository's legal counsel. No matter how records come into the custody of the repository, the archivist must have written documentation that establishes the repository's custodial rights or legal title to the records.

• With jurisdictional custody, the archivist also becomes responsible for the care of the records. The archivist should take physical custody of the records in a timely fashion, make them accessible, and ensure their preservation until such time as they are fully arranged and described. To do this, archivists must provide a basic level of control, both for the physical records themselves and information about them.

• The selection process generates important basic information about an accession. This information should be integrated into a "process control" system so that it can be utilized for many subsequent archival functions ranging from arrangement, description, and access to storage, preservation, and statistical accounting.

Selected Readings

Fredric M. Miller, *Arranging and Describing Archives and Manuscripts,* Archival Fundamental Series (Chicago: Society of American Archivists, 1990), 31–44.

Trudy Huskamp Peterson, "The Gift and the Deed," *American Archivist* 42 (January 1979), 61–66.

Gary M. Peterson and Trudy Huskamp Peterson, *Archives & Manuscripts: Law* (Chicago: Society of American Archivists, 1985), 11–38.

Dennis F. Walle, "The Deposit Agreement in Archival Collection Development," *The Midwestern Archivist* 10 (1985), 117–27.

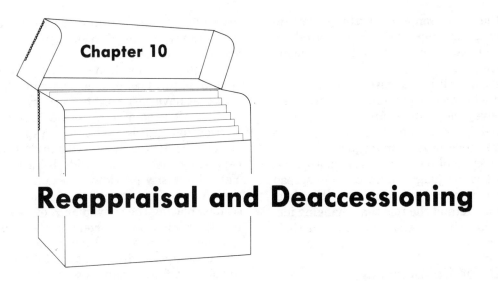

Reappraisal and Deaccessioning

Until the 1980s, reappraisal and deaccessioning were considered the antithesis of building a documentary heritage, if they were thought about at all. Recently, however, many archivists have come to realize that a systematic and continuing procedure to reevaluate past appraisal and acquisition decisions is essential to developing a program with strong, well-focused holdings that makes wise use of preservation resources. Deaccessioning, as Lawrence Dowler notes, is a "legitimate function of appraisal" and "an essential part of collection development."[1]

Why We Need to Reappraise and Deaccession

There are few, if any, repositories that do not have collections that would not be accepted today. Some collections are fragmentary, others possess redundant information, and still more are irrelevant to the institution's mission. Many repositories are awash with records acquired without ever having been appraised. Such collections may have been accepted because of political considerations; that is, gentle persuasion on the part of donors, academic researchers, trustees, or similar repository guardians. Archivists have also accepted records they did not want in the hopes that the donor would transfer desired material later. If, for any reason, records will not pass appraisal muster today, why should they continue to occupy shelf space? "For such records,"

writes Leonard Rapport, "there should be no grandfather clause."[2]

Every repository . . . has on its shelves records which, if offered today, we would not accept. If we wouldn't accept them today , why should we permit these records to occupy shelf space? For such records there should be no grandfather clause.

Leonard Rapport, "No Grandfather Clause," 1981

The Perils of Deaccessioning

Deaccessioning presents many perils, and, at present, archivists have little literature or previous practice to guide them over its treacherous shoals. Some perils are based on the public's perception of an archives. In the public and academic mind, archives exist to collect and preserve records, not to destroy them (though that is a primary goal of appraisal). Archivists who carry out reappraisal are often viewed as barbarians who put crass considerations of economical management before scholarship and culture. Some perils relate to the public's perception of the archivist's responsibility. Archivists rightly fear that an incensed donor, heir, or researcher, proclaiming that valuable records have been disposed of, will jeopardize the repository's acquisitions program.

---

[1] Lawrence Dowler, "Deaccessioning Collections: A New Perspective on a Continuing Controversy," in Peace (ed.), *Archival Choices*, 117.

[2] Leonard Rapport, "No Grandfather Clause: Reappraising Accessioned Records," *American Archivist* 44 (Spring 1981), 143.

Within the profession, some archivists regard deaccessioning as an "invitation to a bonfire" by those who would cavalierly overturn the judgments of their predecessors.[3]

The greatest peril is that historical fashion or ideology could wipe out aspects of the historical record as successive generations of archivists erase the decisions of their predecessors. Just as more archivists' saving more records in more places spreads the burden of documentary preservation in a spatial sense, different value judgments over time spread this burden in a temporal way. Archivists, therefore, must clearly understand the role that changing ideology and fashions in research may play in their reappraisal decisions.

The Benefits of Reappraisal

Reappraisal is a collection management tool for correcting flawed appraisal decisions of the past or changing those that are no longer valid. While many records merit indefinite retention, few are eternal and deserve permanent preservation. Reappraisal makes the archives a living organism in which those records that prove to be of little value are allowed to perish. This process permits the archivist to strengthen and refine holdings. Records of lesser value can be replaced with collections of greater significance. Frequently, the information in some earlier acquisitions will be made redundant by subsequent, richer acquisitions. Most important, reappraisal can prevent archivists from imposing the necessarily tentative and often imperfect decisions of the past on the future.

Types of Deaccessioning

• *Destruction.* Outright destruction is the most suitable method of disposition for most reappraised records that do not merit continued preservation, particularly governmental or other institutional archives. But deaccessioning is not always synonymous with destruction and does not always involve the disposal of worthless records. It takes place in many ways.

• *Transfer to a more appropriate depository.* In reappraising holdings, archivists often come upon random bits and pieces of out-of-scope material—a few letters, a broadside, some photographs and so forth—which they often deaccession and send to a more appropriate repository. This collegial and commonsense type of deaccessioning is a well-established archival practice.

Going an important step further, archivists can reunite natural collections or organic bodies of records that have been split between two or more institutions, often as a result of an ill-informed or ill-advised donor decision. Reuniting split collections is one deaccessioning variant that archivists not handicapped by institutional pride have long practiced. Yale University provides an example of such practice. Yale's Department of Archives and Manuscripts, placing the convenience of researchers over institutional pride, transferred a few boxes of correspondence from Yale alumnus Senator Robert A. Taft to a larger collection at the Library of Congress so the Taft family papers would be accessible as a unit.[4]

In today's archival acquisition environment, archivists need to move beyond these simple and obvious types of record transfers and systematically identify valuable out-of-scope collections that merit preservation in more appropriate homes. Transfer of records usually poses few political concerns and is a satisfying solution to the problem of saving out-of-scope material.

• *Sale.* Out-of-scope items of monetary value may be disposed of by sale, an accepted practice used by libraries and museums, one which should also be adopted by the prudent archival manager. Sale items may include autographed letters, stock certificates, rare imprints, maps, and photographs which are either duplicate or have little or no informational or intrinsic value to the repository. In disposing of such items, the repository will generally be best served by using a reputable manuscripts and rare book dealer. To buffer any criticism that may arise from the sale of deaccessioned items, most repositories restrict the use of sale proceeds to maintenance of the remaining collections.[5]

Collections must be administered and preserved, but not as if they were sacraments. Responsible curators, archivists and librarians must constantly interpret and evaluate their collections as forces in a collection plan, and not as a part of immutable law sanctioned by Holy Writ.

Lawrence Dowler, "Deaccessioning Collections," 1984

---

[3] See Karen Benedict, "Invitation to a Bonfire: Reappraisal and Deaccessioning of Records as Collection Management Tools in an Archives—A Reply to Leonard Rapport," *American Archivist* 47 (Winter 1984), 43–49.

[4] Dowler, "Deaccessioning Collections," 119.
[5] For a reappraisal case study, see Richard L. Haas, "Collection Reappraisal: The Experience at the University of Cincinnati," *American Archivist* 47 (Winter 1984), 51–54.

Figure 10-1 Deaccessioning Policy

State Historical Society of Wisconsin
Policy for Deaccessioning Materials from the Library and Archives Collections

Introduction

Until recently, research institutions had relatively few constraints on space, staff and other resources and were able to pursue broad collecting programs that were often ill-defined or indiscriminate. Today, the sheer volume, cost and complexity of research materials, whether books and pamphlets, records and papers or photographs and magnetic recordings force archivists and librarians to take a more selective and focused approach to building collections. Part of this approach is the development of well-articulated collecting policies and plans. An important element of a collections policy is deaccessioning—the disposal of materials from the collections through sale, transfer to other institutions or destruction.

For archives and libraries, deaccessioning is an integral and essential tool of collections management. The State Historical Society has deaccessioned materials since its inception, when Lyman Copeland Draper routinely exchanged duplicate gifts with other institutions in order to build the fledgling collections. This deaccession policy clarifies and formalizes the practices of the last 140 years; by adhering to its principles, staff will more efficiently fulfill the Society's mission of preserving and disseminating information to its patrons.

The policy statement specifies the criteria to be considered when the State Historical Society of Wisconsin desires to dispose of items in the Library and Archives collections (including all material accessioned, whether processed or not) which have substantial research or financial value and outlines the methods to be employed when deaccessioning takes place. It does *not* pertain to the ordinary functions of collections management, such as the routine weeding of archival or book collections according to accepted practice. Rather, this statement is intended to ensure the proper disposition of those materials which have substantial research or monetary value and yet are inappropriate for the Society's collections.

Evaluation of Materials

Before deaccessioning materials with substantial research or financial value, the following questions will be considered by professional staff and the head librarian or state archivist, and an appraisal report will be completed and reviewed by the head librarian or state archivist.

1. Does the material fall within the scope of current collecting policies?
2. Is the material a duplicate or does it duplicate information already held in the collections in another format?
3. Has the material deteriorated beyond real usefulness?
4. Do any externally imposed restrictions such as donor agreements or government depository arrangements apply to the material?
5. How would deaccessioning the material affect public access to information?

Disposition of Materials

Section 44.015(2) of the Wisconsin Statutes provides that the Society may "sell, exchange or otherwise dispose of" duplicate materials or materials outside its fields of collections. In practice, material to be deaccessioned may be transferred to other scholarly institutions, offered for public sale or destroyed. Any such disposition of material with substantial research or financial value will be governed by the following considerations:

1. Materials must be free of all legal impediments. There will be no deaccessioning of such materials when this action is contrary to any written agreement between the Society and the donor. Reasonable attempts will be made to consult donors when materials are considered for deaccessioning.
2. Before materials of substantial research or financial value are deaccessioned, reasonable attempts will be made to determine if other Society collecting units have an interest in them.
3. No private sales or gifts of such materials will be made to Society staff, to the Board of Curators or to members of their immediate families.
4. All proceeds from the sale of such materials will be used solely to further the preservation or development of the Society's research collections.
5. The method of disposition will be decided jointly by the appropriate professional staff, the head librarian or state archivist and the Assistant Director for Research Services.
6. When deaccessioning is determined appropriate according to the foregoing considerations, responsibility for disposition will be as follows: materials valued at less than $1,000 may be deaccessioned at the discretion of the professional staff after consultation with the head librarian or state archivist; those valued at $1,000 to $5,000 will require the additional approval of the Assistant Director for Research Services and the Director of the Society; those valued at more than $5,000 will be referred to the Board of Curators for their approval, at the discretion of the Society's Director.

Approved by the Board of Curators February 22, 1986.

Safeguards in Deaccessioning

Generally, the same criteria an institution uses to select new acquisitions are applied to reappraise accessioned records. While the archivist will often serendipitously, come across an isolated item, series, or even collection of the most dubious value to the repository, for the most part reappraisal should not be done on a piecemeal basis but carried out as an on-going process. When appraising incoming records, for example, the archivist should reexamine related records already accessioned within the same or other record groups. Older, unprocessed accessions should be reappraised before the arrangement and description process begins. Rapport advocates reappraisal, based on the use of the records, at periodic intervals,"perhaps twenty, twenty-five, or thirty years." Whatever the merits of such an approach, it is inherently dangerous if it is based exclusively on short-term use of the records.[6]

Because the impact of a deaccessioning decision, particularly a controversial one, can be much more widespread and detrimental to the collecting program than the rejection of a proposed new accession, archivists must have safeguards that will protect the institution and its staff and program from any political or other fall-out.

The first and most basic safeguard is a written policy statement governing the process which sets forth the scope of the program, the evaluation and review process, and the conditions that must be met prior to any deaccession. This policy should be approved by the repository's highest authority.

Most deaccession actions should undergo the same rigorous review that an incoming accession would receive, including a written reappraisal report that carefully examines the initial appraisal and is approved by the same body that reviews incoming accessions. These decisions need to be meticulously documented and reflect collective judgment.

It is especially important that the archivist be aware of any legal impediments to deaccessioning and that they be resolved prior to taking any action.

It is advisable to have the repository's legal counsel review the transaction. All major deaccession decisions should be approved at the highest executive or governing board level. (See Figure 10-1.)

Some Caveats on Deaccessioning

• Accessioning should not entail an "eternal obligation" on the part of the repository. Records creators and donors must be aware that many factors such as changing mission, other accessions, and financial responsibilities may preclude the perpetual preservation of an accession. The conditional nature of the accession should be clearly stated in the document that gives the repository legal title to the records. Generally, preservation should be "continuing" and not "permanent."

• Reappraisal is a collection management tool to improve holdings and amplify resources. It is an on-going function, not a crisis management weapon used to dismember the archives whenever there is a need for space or money for some purpose.[7]

• While reappraisal is a needed corrective, the archivist's first line of defense is to keep selection policy current and to apply rigorously sound appraisal standards. Good initial appraisal can reduce the need for deaccessioning.

• Deaccessioning should take place in an inter-institutional context to assure that not all archivists dispose of records documenting the same activities.

Selected Readings

Karen Benedict, "Invitation to a Bonfire: Reappraisal and Deaccessioning of Records as Collection Management Tools in an Archives—A Reply to Leonard Rapport," *American Archivist* 47 (Winter 1984), 43–49.

Lawrence Dowler, "Deaccessioning Collections: A New Perspective on a Continuing Controversy," in Peace (ed.), *Archival Choices*, 117–32.

Leonard Rapport, "No Grandfather Clause: Reappraising Accessioned Records," *American Archivist* 44 (Spring 1981), 143–50.

---

[6] Rapport, "No Grandfather Clause," 145; Benedict, "Invitation to a Bonfire," 47–48.

[7] Benedict, "Invitation to a Bonfire," 45.

New Directions in Selection and Appraisal: Broader Contexts, Better Tools

As archivists take a more active role in shaping the historical record, they realize they are handicapped by the lack of tools and the inadequacies of frameworks for record selection. A few archivists have begun to address this shortcoming. This chapter examines some of the new tools and frameworks they have developed.

The first of these is a documentation strategy premised on the assumption that the selection and appraisal of the contemporary record must take place through analysis and planning in a broad, multi-institutional setting. The second is the use of the information systems concept to provide an enlarged context for the appraisal of integrated record systems. The third, sharing appraisal information, attempts to provide a mechanism better to inform appraisal decisions on parallel and related records documenting similar activities and functions among various governmental or organizational hierarchies. The fourth, appraisal methodology, provides an expanded and precisely defined taxonomy of appraisal criteria which can also be numerically weighted to further inform the evaluation process.[1]

Documentation Strategies

A growing chorus of archivists claims that institutionally focused selection cannot alone deal with the volume and complexity of modern records. They argue that the multi-institutional nature and inter-disciplinary study of today's institutions, issues, and events require a selection process in which institutions plan and coordinate acquisition activities so that each can save a different segment of a larger documentary record. The proponents claim that without inter-institutional coordination, archivists risk needless replication about some aspects of a subject, while retaining nothing about other important aspects. According to the SAA Goals and Priorities Task Force report, *Planning for the Archival Profession,* documentation strategies will enable "archivists to study selected portions of the complex record . . . which transcend the concern of any one repository," and thereby "foster the integration and coordination of collecting programs." Most important, it "will help archivists to compile a more balanced and representative record of Society."[2]

What is a documentation strategy? According to the conceptual model's principal architects, Helen Samuels, Archivist at Massachusetts Institute of Technology, and Larry J. Hackman, New York State Archives and Records Administration, it is a "**plan** formulated to assure the adequate documentation of an on-going issue, activity, function, or subject."[3]

---

[1] This chapter is based in part on the author's unpublished paper, "Documenting Our Times: The Archivist's Search for New Methodologies," presented at a plenary session of the Midwest Archives Conference, Columbia, Missouri, October 17, 1987. The author also has made liberal use of Margaret Hedstrom's excellent article, "New Appraisal Techniques: The Effect of Theory on Practice," *Provenance* 7:2 (Fall 1989), 2–21.

[2] *Planning for the Archival Profession,* 10.

[3] Helen W. Samuels, "Who Controls the Past" *American Archivist* 49 (Spring 1986), 109–24; Larry J. Hackman and Joan Warnow-Blewett, "The Documentary Strategy Process: A Model and a Case Study," *American Archivist* 50 (Winter 1987), 12–47; Larry J. Hackman, "The Forum," *American Archivist* 52 (Winter 1989), 8–9.

Documentation strategies are an analytic and planned approach to solving problems posed by modern documentation. The key elements encompassed in this approach are an analysis of the universe to be documented, an understanding of the inherent documentary problems, and the formulation of a plan to assure the documentation of an ongoing issue, activity, or geographic area. The strategy is ordinarily designed, promoted, and in part implemented by an ongoing mechanism involving records creators, administrators (including archivists), and users. The documentation strategy is carried out through the mutual efforts of many institutions and individuals influencing the creation of records, the archival retention of a portion of them, and the development of sufficient resources to carry out the cooperative preservation effort. The strategy is refined in response to changing conditions and viewpoints.

Lewis & Lynn Lady Bellardo, *A Glossary for Archivists, Manuscript Curators, and Records Managers,* 1992

The documentary process starts by evaluating what functions and activities should be documented and envisioning the kinds of information required to document those functions and activities, rather than beginning with what records exist or should be kept. It is "designed, promoted, and in part implemented by an **on-going mechanism** involving archival documentation creators, records administrators, archivists, users, other experts, and beneficiaries and other interested parties."

Documentation strategies recognize the multi-institutional and interdisciplinary nature of issues and events and the interrelatedness of the resulting record. Appraisal, therefore, requires a joint analysis by all concerned. This analysis takes into consideration such factors as what evidence is needed to document a given event or subject and what is the full range or universe of the documentation, published or unpublished, textual and visual. Archivists and their colleagues use this knowledge to develop an acquisitions plan.

The "strategy is carried out through the **mutual efforts** of many institutions and individuals influencing the creation and management of records and the retention and archival accessioning of some of them." This requires interinstitutional cooperation and resource sharing. Institutions must be willing to cooperate in carrying out the acquisitions plan and accessioning relevant records. Note that documentation strategies do not necessarily create new repositories but rather rely on existing archives. Archivists need to understand how their holdings not only document their own institution but how they might contribute information important to a variety of documentation strategies. The concept thus provides archivists with a new way of looking at their institutional holdings.

The last element of a documentation strategy is monitoring and updating the plan. The "strategy is **regularly refined** in response to changing conditions as reflected in available information, expertise and opinions."[4] Because modern records are voluminous, affected by rapidly changing information technologies, and created in multi-institutional settings, there needs to be a mechanism for continuous monitoring of records creation, management, and appraisal. Documentation strategy can be applied in most settings, whether it is to document a subject, a functional area, or a political or geographical unit. A parallel analytical process, under the label of "institutional functional analysis" can also be applied at the level of the individual organization.[5]

Conceptually, the process offers many advantages:

- it gives archivists the ability to appraise and select interrelated records across institutional and disciplinary boundaries and thereby determine what and where is the best or fullest record of an activity. Because it is a pro-active plan, archivists will not have to select from what chance and accident have left behind.

- it enables archivists to deal comprehensively with a mass of interrelated records, thus systematically reducing overlapping and duplicate documentation. It also maximizes resources available for archival selection and preservation.

- it provides a framework in which archivists can influence record creators to provide a more adequate social documentation.

- it better serves the interests of researchers by identifying and filling gaps in the historical record.

---

[4] Hackman and Warnow-Blewett, "The Documentation Strategy Process," 14. Emphasis added.
[5] See page 17.

In spite of the concept's intellectual attraction, it faces major obstacles in implementation.[6] The documentation strategy construct is untested. Some models are sophisticated beyond current archival capabilities and depend on highly speculative cooperation. Other models have a *modus operandi* that is too complex and overly bureaucratic.[7] The support structures and mechanisms needed for interinstitutional information exchange and for planning and implementation of documentation strategies have yet to be developed. Nevertheless, archivists are attempting to apply the concepts on a limited basis. A particularly important effort is the SAA Congressional Roundtable's work to develop a plan for documenting the federal Congress. The usefulness of the concept in developing documentation plans hinges on such testing and application.

Two obstacles that documentation strategy faces, however, will be difficult to overcome. The first is intellectual, defining what functions and activities need to be documented in the universe of human activity. The second is fiscal, securing the resources to develop and carry out the acquisition plans. Unless archivists use the model only as an acquisition plan for occasional or very specific interinstitutional archival selection efforts, they will literally need a "universe of [interrelated] documentation strategies" to make sure important activities and subjects do not go undocumented or to avoid overlapping and conflicting strategies.

While documentation strategies are designed to conserve and amplify resources, critics see the economics of implementation as an insurmountable problem. With inadequate resources for traditional institution-based appraisal, where are the resources for this complex interinstitutional appraisal? Documentary strategists need to develop a cost-benefit analysis that will tell archivists when it is worthwhile to invest the human effort and financial resources necessary to plan and implement these often complex and long-term procedures.

The model, observes one writer, "is not a strategy as much as it is a Sangreal—the Holy Grail."[8]

For Samuels, that is not bad. At present, she believes "the primary value of the documentation strategy model seems to be the broad discussion it has generated about how the archival heritage is assembled."[9] The model makes three important contributions to current discussions and ongoing research in the archival selection process. **One,** intelligent selection requires that archivists understand the interrelatedness of institutions, their functions and activities, and the records they create. **Two,** because of this interrelatedness, archivists need to cooperate with other records creators and custodians in developing an acquisitions plan to implement specific collection policy goals. **Three,** archivists need to focus first on what functions and activities need to be documented and then, through the appraisal process, select the best records from a larger universe of available information. As an applied methodology, the concept may prove most useful in developing documentation policies and plans at the institutional level.

The Information Systems Concept: A Framework for the Appraisal of Integrated Records Systems

Modern records are increasingly created and distributed as part of integrated and often complex electronic information systems with multiple input sources, shared databases, and various output formats. In these systems, information is stored and distributed both electronically and in hard copy. For these information systems the traditional context and unit of appraisal—the record function and series—are inadequate for analysis. Margaret Hedstrom, the head of the analysis and disposition bureau at the New York State Archives and Records Administration, argues that archivists need to exploit the information systems concept as a framework and tool for selection when dealing with the documentary products of modern information processing technology.[10] This concept, developed by systems analysts and information scientists, has provided a basic framework for the design and development of recordkeeping systems for two decades and today many records are organized as part of an information system.

Appraising these systems, according to Hedstrom, is a challenge to archivists. Because the structure of such an information system does not always

[6] For brief critiques of documentation strategies, see David Bearman, "Archival Methods," 13–15; Frank Boles, "Mix Two Parts Interest to One Part Information," 363–65; and Frank Boles, "Commentary" on Richard J. Cox and Helen W. Samuels, "The Archivist's First Responsibility: A Research Agenda to Improve the Identification and Retention of Records of Enduring Value," *American Archivist* 51 (Winter and Spring 1988), 43–46.

[7] See Hackman and Warnow-Blewett, "The Documentary Strategy Process: A Model and a Case Study," 12–47.

[8] Terry Abraham, "Collection Policy or Documentation Strategy: Theory and Practice," *American Archivist* 54 (Winter 1991), 44–52.

[9] Cox and Samuels, "The Archivist's First Responsibility," 40.

[10] This section is drawn from Hedstrom, "New Appraisal Techniques," 16–20.

parallel that of the office or organization it serves, archivists do not have the familiar provenance-based landmarks of record function to guide them. Information systems can bridge several units within an agency and transmit data from one agency to another. Some of the networks are very complex. Hedstrom uses the example of the national criminal records system, which transfers information on a variety of related activities both vertically among federal, state, and local officials, and horizontally among similar agencies within and between states. Information systems usually contain records in both manual files and electronic databases. The record may be a custodial orphan that is combined with other data in a corporatewide shared database, where the information "belongs to everyone and no one." Further, she notes, archivists unfamiliar with automated records systems tend to treat the hard-copy outputs such as computer generated reports and correspondence not as components of the system, but as traditional paper-based records and files. This approach, says Hedstrom, obscures how the records were created, their relationship to other types of documentation, and the "impact of automation on the organization, conceptualization, and use of information."

The information systems approach offers the archivist a manageable way to analyze complex multi-institutional records systems.

• The systems design, specifications, diagrams of information flow, and other documentation help archivists understand the purpose of these modern records and the impact of automation on their organization and use.

• The systems design defines the relationship between the various forms of documentation such as source documents, data sets, and output reports. It tells the archivist how information flows among the various systems users and often provides information about how hard-copy output is generated and distributed.

• The approach provides an economical way to analyze voluminous and complex interrelated records as a total system rather than on a traditional series component basis.

To be effective, the information systems approach requires archival intervention at the system's creation. The archivist should prepare a comprehensive documentation plan even before any records are generated. In preparing the plan, the archivist needs to meet with records creators and

users to define what electronic and hard copy elements merit retention. The archivist must also develop a set of criteria that systems designers can use to identify what information in the system has long-term value. Further, the archivist must make sure that routines are built into the system to control records retention and disposition as well as the preservation of selected archival material. Finally, where many agencies and governmental jurisdictions share and use the data, the archivist should develop a collaborative appraisal assessment.

Where information systems exist appraisal archivists can take advantage of the pre-defined parameters of a system and the explicit relationships among its components to provide a framework for analysis of complex multi-institutional records.

Margaret Hedstrom, "New Appraisal Techniques," 1989

The appraisal framework provided by the information systems concept is not experimental, but the archivist has to make it operational. What the profession needs now are more case studies demonstrating the method and techniques of information systems appraisal such as the recent appraisal of the New York State computerized criminal history system.[11]

Sharing Information about Appraisal Decisions

Sharing information about appraisal decisions, now being tested by government records archivists, is another approach to providing a larger context for selection. In carrying out similar functions such as banking and securities regulation, public safety, and consumer protection, state governments create similar records. This kind of documentary replication also occurs when the same function—equal rights litigation for example—is exercised by local, state, and national authorities and results in similar information. In the private sector, whether in business, labor, or service and social organizations, there is documentary replication on much the same scale. Lacking information about how their colleagues nationwide reach appraisal decisions in similar areas, archivists make their selections in a vacuum.

---

[11] See Alan Kowlowitz, "Archival Appraisal of Online Information Systems," *Archives and Museum Informatics* 2 (Fall 1988).

With a mechanism to share information about appraisal decisions, archivists could select records in a more informed context. A staff of a state archival repository, for example, might keep a particular series such as the "domestic" or in-state insurance company annual reports after they learned that the series was also held by most states, thus preserving a comprehensive nationwide record of insurance company activity at the state level. On the other hand, the same staff might conclude from the appraisal decision of other state archivists that the function of licensing bingo—a minor activity in their state—is adequately documented elsewhere and recommend destruction of the records.[12] An intergovernmental example is the periodic reports of FDIC-member banks, which are filed with both the state commissioner of banking and the Federal Deposit Insurance Corporation. If appraisers also know that the federal copy is scheduled for transfer to the National Archives, they can more skillfully weigh the merits of local retention.[13]

There are major obstacles to be overcome before shared appraisal information becomes a useful and affordable tool. The fragmentary database of information about governmental records needs to be enlarged to provide a reliable context of appraisal information. The lack of descriptive consistency as well as the generally vague and inadequate information repositories provide about the appraisal decision-making process limits the technique's usefulness. More work is needed in developing standards for describing public records and deciding what data elements must be included in on-line systems to make appraisal information meaningful and comparable. Appraisers also need to determine when it is useful to share appraisal decisions.[14]

Beyond these problems, the day-to-day usefulness of this approach is untested. An interinstitutional context is unnecessary for most appraisal deci-sions. An appraiser does not need national information when records are retained to meet specific institutional mandates. A state archives will retain the board minutes of its department of natural resources for their evidential value regardless of decisions by other states on conservation matters.

An on-line system (RLIN) is being used in a very preliminary and simple way. At present, it primarily provides a starting point in determining what institutions to contact for more detailed appraisal information such as copies of schedules or appraisal memoranda. The National Archives, in a rudimentary step to facilitate the shared appraisal process, has set up a telephone number to handle inquiries about records scheduled by NARA.[15]

A national archival on-line database is a uniquely powerful tool for the sharing of data about intergovernmental records, surpassing all current finding aid systems in inclusiveness and retrieval power.

Intergovernmental Records Project: Phase I Report, 1990

While sharing information about appraisal decisions can help archivists avoid duplication of effort when appraising parallel or related sets of records, it is not a substitute for independent archival judgment. While it can inform a decision, shared appraisal rarely should be the sole factor in the decision. The process also can easily lend itself to propagating a bad decision by fostering copycat selection. Only the repository archivist can decide when a similar set of records provides redundant information or important comparative documentation and whether the records should be retained to meet local imperatives or destroyed because they are preserved in another jurisdiction.

As has already been suggested, the greatest promise of shared appraisal information is in appraising records retained for their broader informational value in an intergovernmental or other vertically structured records program. Archivists in different jurisdictions need to collaborate not only to determine what should be preserved but to put in place agreements specifying who will be responsible for what segment of the records. As these programs develop, archivists need to take the process an important step further and compile information for researchers about the extent of interjurisdictional records in any given area that are available for

---

[12] Max J. Evans, "The Visible Hand: Creating a Practical Mechanism for Cooperative Appraisal," *The Midwestern Archivist* 11 (1986), 7–13.

[13] Sharing appraisal information about records documenting parallel activities among the states is one of the goals of the Research Libraries Group's Government Records Project, involving thirteen state archival agencies and the District of Columbia. This group is cooperating with the National Archives' pilot Intergovernmental Records Project, which is studying the hierarchical relationship of those intergovernmental records that contain duplicate information, relate to parallel functions, or result from federal programs carried out by lower governmental units. National Archives and Records Administration, *The Intergovernmental Records Project: Phase I Report* (Washington: National Archives and Records Administration, 1990), 1–36.

[14] The Research Libraries Group, "Seven States Archives Project: Final Report on Year Two of the Project," (Stanford 1988).

[15] *Intergovernmental Records Project: Phase I Report,* 36. The National Archives and Records Administration telephone number is (202) 501-6040.

Figure 11-1   Value-of-Information Module

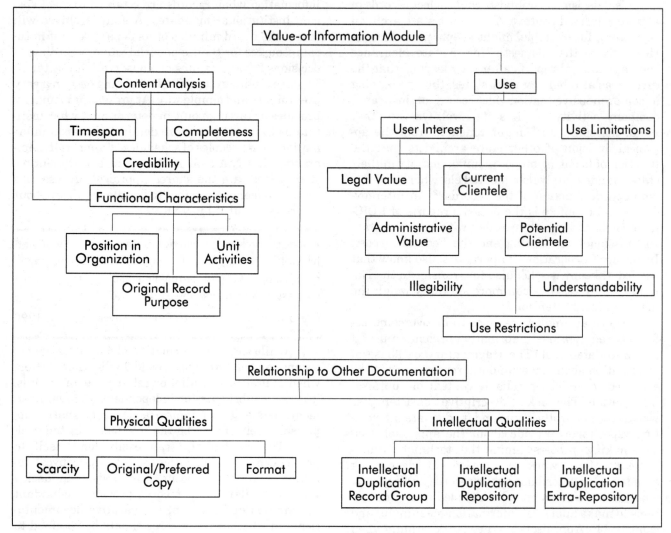

research. Sharing information about appraisal decisions will be an important element of any interinstitutional documentary strategy or plan.

Defining the Selection Process: A Taxonomy for Appraisal

The need for agreed-upon selection standards, methods, and terminology so evident in the shared appraisal projects is the focus of research conducted by Frank Boles in association with Julia Marks Young. In *Archival Appraisal* (1991) they have developed a model, based on a matrix of appraisal criteria, which they believe will bring "consistency, consensus, and more rigorous analysis" to the selection process. At present, the authors believe, archivists lack adequate tools for selection, both at the policy or macro-selection level—what information an institu-

tion should collect—and at the micro-selection level—what records best meet policy-level needs. While the study concentrates on the development of micro-level tools—appraisal criteria—used to shape the archival record, these tools can only be properly used when linked to macro-level tools such as accession policies, whether in setting the parameters for a collecting repository or an institutional archives. Without policy, there is no focus or boundary to the body of information in the archives; without the tools to select records with appropriate information, the selection process results in documents on a subject assembled by happenstance and intuition. Selection tools are essential to implement policy.[16]

---

[16] Boles, *Archival Appraisal,* 97–98, 101–03. Also see Boles, "Mix Two Parts Interest to One Part Information," 356–68 for a discussion of the interrelationship of these tools and their policy implications.

Archivists have not created a well-defined methodology to govern selection. This failure has created a situation in which archivists possess a variety of selection tools and policies, but no clear sense about when particular tools are applied, how the tools interrelate, or how policy and tools should interact.

Frank Boles, *Archival Appraisal,* 1991

To organize appraisal criteria and apply them more systematically, Boles and Young have formulated a "complete appraisal taxonomy" that divides some fifty criteria into three modules or matrices. The first, the **value of the information module,** examines records in terms of their functional characteristics, their importance as information resources, their physical and intellectual uniqueness, and their use potential and limitations. (See Figure 11-1.) The **cost of retention module** evaluates the expense of records acquisition, processing, preservation/conservation, storage, and reference. Where the first two represent fairly traditional concerns within the selection process, the **implications of the selection decision module** articulates for the first time the impact a selection decision may have upon both internal and external policy. Internally, for example, what effect will an acquisition have upon subsequent acquisition decisions—does it change the rules? Externally, how would the political fallout of a selection decision unpopular with users and/or donors impact upon other institutional policies? The evaluative criteria in this module are preliminary and tentative.[17]

Young and Boles believe the archival community "is approaching a common definition of selection tools," and now needs to develop a "consistent method" for applying them. Developing such a methodology is their second major objective. One key to its development is the use of numerical methods to "better express the exact nature and strength" of a record's evaluation. The authors believe that quantitative approaches will not only improve archivists' understanding of why particular records are selected and assist them in applying this understanding in a more "consistent and even-handed manner," but also help "define archivists' image among non-archivists" by demonstrating the "unique judgments which archivists claim fall within their sphere of professional responsibilities." By rationalizing ar-

chival judgment, the authors believe numerical selection systems will prove a very beneficial tool.[18]

Boles and Young also point out that there are several "hidden prejudices or biases" implicit in archival selection criteria. For example, selection based on evidential values is structurally biased against non-elites. A second key to a consistent application of the appraisal criteria is to understand and eliminate these biases. The authors think the psychological and sociological literature on decision-making "may serve as a springboard for understanding and eliminating" these hidden biases.

The Boles-Young study stresses the fundamental role of institutional selection policies in acquisition decisions and the importance of linking record selection criteria to this policy in order to translate policy goals into "appropriate information found in real records." In defining and integrating the criteria needed to evaluate records, they have developed a tool that should enable archivists to make more rigorous and comparable selection decisions. To some readers, the authors' ideas may seem arcane if not utopian; nevertheless, the project is a thoughtful research agenda for further work on the archival selection process.[19]

Summary

This chapter is one of promise, not performance, and as such is an anomaly in a manual of practice. Yet it underscores some of the main currents in this volume: the technical complexity, organizational interrelatedness, and mass of modern records; and the resultant need for more systematic selection processes and expanded selection frameworks as well as economical methods for selecting less and less from more and more. In time, some of the tools outlined in this chapter may assist the archivist toward such goals, At present, however, with the exception of the systems approach to appraising complex information systems, none of these tools is operational. If they are to become operational it will take further research, testing, refinement, and, above all, resources. While lacking immediate applicability for the practicing appraiser, these selection models show that archivists, as they approach the twenty-first century, are devoting much of their intellectual capital to their most demanding task.

---

[17] This taxonomy was first developed in Boles and Young, "Exploring the Black Box: The Appraisal of University Administrative Records," 121–58.

[18] Boles, *Archival Appraisal,* 89, 99.
[19] Ibid., 101–03.

Selected Readings

Philip N. Alexander and Helen W. Samuels, "The Roots of 128: A Hypothetical Documentation Strategy," *American Archivist* 50 (Fall 1987), 518–31.

Frank Boles in association with Julia Marks Young, *Archival Appraisal* (New York: Neal-Schuman Publishers, Inc., 1991).

Richard J. Cox and Helen W. Samuels, "The Archivist's First Responsibility: A Research Agenda to Improve the Identification and Retention of Records of Enduring Value," *American Archivist* 51 (Winter and Spring 1988), 28–42.

Max J. Evans, "The Visible Hand: Creating a Practical Mechanism for Cooperative Appraisal," *Midwestern Archivist* 11 (1986), 7–13.

Larry J. Hackman and Joan Warnow-Blewett, "The Documentary Strategy Process: A Model and a Case Study," *American Archivist* 50 (Winter 1987), 12–47.

Margaret Hedstrom, "New Appraisal Techniques: The Effect of Theory on Practice," *Provenance* 7:2 (Fall 1989), 1–21.

National Archives and Records Administration, *Intergovernmental Records Project: Phase I Report* (Washington: National Archives, July 1990).

Helen Willa Samuels, "Who Controls the Past," *American Archivist* 49 (Spring 1986), 109–24.

Index